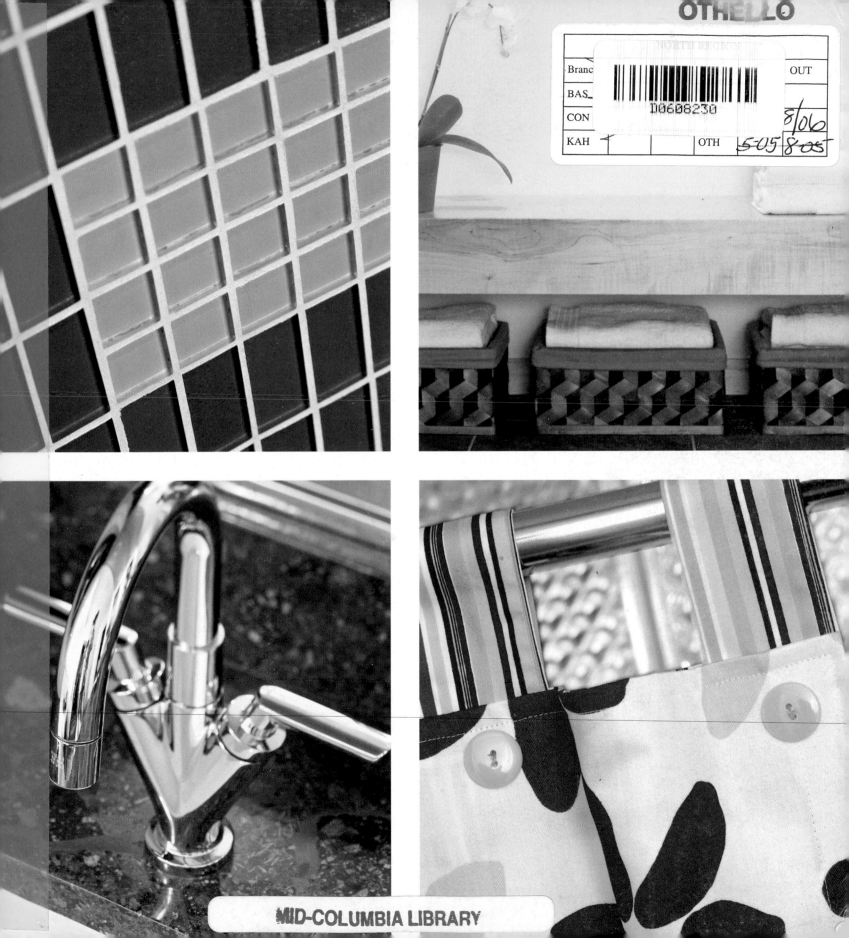

HGTV BATHS

EDITOR: Amy Tincher-Durik
SENIOR ASSOCIATE DESIGN DIRECTOR: Doug Samuelson
PROJECT EDITORS AND WRITERS: Amber Dawn Barz, Jan Soults Walker
CONTRIBUTING ART DIRECTORS Chris Conyers, Beth Runcie, Joe Wysong (Conyers Design, Inc.)
COPY CHIEF: Terri Fredrickson
PUBLISHING OPERATIONS MANAGER: Karen Schirm
EDIT AND DESIGN PRODUCTION COORDINATOR: Mary Lee Gavin
EDITORIAL ASSISTANTS: Kaye Chabot, Kairee Mullen
MARKETING PRODUCT MANAGERS: Aparna Pande, Isaac Petersen, Gina Rickert, Stephen Rogers, Brent Wiersma, Tyler Woods
BOOK PRODUCTION MANAGERS: Pam Kvitne, Marjorie J. Schenkelberg, Rick von Holdt, Mark Weaver
CONTRIBUTING STYLISTS: Cathy Kramer (Cathy Kramer Designs), Robin Tucker
PHOTOGRAPHERS: Edmund Barr, John Ellis, Michael Garland, Ken Gutmaker, Andy Lyons, Cameron Sadeghpour
CONTRIBUTING COPY EDITOR: Stacey Schildroth
CONTRIBUTING PROOFREADERS: Pam Elizian, Becky Etchen, Nancy Ruhling
ILLUSTRATOR: Chad Johnston, Tom Stocki (The Art Factory)
INDEXER: Kathleen Poole

MEREDITH® BOOKS

EXECUTIVE DIRECTOR, EDITORIAL: Gregory H. Kayko
EXECUTIVE DIRECTOR, DESIGN: Matt Strelecki
EXECUTIVE EDITOR/GROUP MANAGER: Denise L. Caringer

PUBLISHER AND EDITOR IN CHIEF: James D. Blume
EDITORIAL DIRECTOR: Linda Raglan Cunningham
EXECUTIVE DIRECTOR, MARKETING: Jeffrey B. Myers
EXECUTIVE DIRECTOR, NEW BUSINESS DEVELOPMENT: Todd M. Davis
EXECUTIVE DIRECTOR, SALES: Ken Zagor
DIRECTOR, OPERATIONS: George A. Susral
DIRECTOR, PRODUCTION: Douglas M. Johnston
BUSINESS DIRECTOR: Jim Leonard

VICE PRESIDENT AND GENERAL MANAGER: Douglas J. Guendel

MEREDITH PUBLISHING GROUP

PRESIDENT: Jack Griffin
SENIOR VICE PRESIDENT: Bob Mate

MEREDITH CORPORATION

CHAIRMAN AND CHIEF EXECUTIVE OFFICER: William T. Kerr
PRESIDENT AND CHIEF OPERATING OFFICER: Stephen M. Lacy

IN MEMORIAM: E.T. Meredith III (1933–2003)

All of us at Meredith® Books are dedicated to providing you with information and ideas to enhance your home. We welcome your comments and suggestions. Write to us at: Meredith Books, Home Decorating and Design Editorial Department, 1716 Locust St., Des Moines, IA 50309-3023.

If you would like to purchase any of our home decorating and design, cooking, crafts, gardening, or home improvement books, check wherever quality books are sold. Or visit us at: meredithbooks.com.

For more information on the topics included in this book and HGTV's shows, visit HGTV.com.

![HGTV HOME & GARDEN TELEVISION]

BATHS

MEREDITH® BOOKS
DES MOINES, IOWA

CONTENTS

PAGE 16

PAGE 32

PAGE 110

INTRODUCTION

PAGE 20

Everyone starts and ends his or her day with a trip to the bath, yet this room is often the most stylistically and spatially neglected place in the home. With the help of this idea- and project-filled guide, you can turn this necessary room into a functional work of art.

FROM SELECTING THE MOST EFFICIENT PLAN to fit your needs and determining a decorating style to choosing surfaces (including flooring, countertops, and backsplashes) and calculating costs, you'll find everything you need in this value-packed bath guide. Information on the latest bath fixtures, cabinetry, and design strategies from top designers featured on HGTV as well as interior designers, architects, and master builders from across the country also is included. Lush color photographs of new and remodeled baths, including some awe-inspiring before and after transformations decorated in myriad styles, will give you the motivation to complete your own bath makeover.

HGTV Baths is divided into the following sections:

A BATH FOR EVERY NEED

Baths are composed of similar fixtures—a sink, a toilet, and a tub or shower (or both)—but different layouts serve different needs. If you share your bath with other family members, a compartmentalized plan may be the answer to your needs; however, if you design the bath just for you, extra doors and privacy alcoves may feel unnecessarily confining. This section shows you a multitude of bath plans that serve various functions, including baths tailored for children, those that serve as a couple's retreat, and those that incorporate accessibility features.

Whatever your needs you will find the right bath design for your lifestyle. Floor plans and planning guidelines are also included to make tailoring your bath easy and efficient.

A BATH FOR EVERY STYLE

Close your eyes and envision the bath of your dreams. Are there spalike amenities to sooth your muscles and your spirit? Do cushy chairs, a coffee bar, and fine furniture cabinets beckon you to come in and relax? Regardless of which style you desire—old-fashioned, contemporary, resort spa, or anything in between—this collection of baths will inspire you. You will learn about the fixtures and materials that complement each style and get expert advice on achieving a personalized look for your bath.

PROJECTS FOR YOUR BATH

If you enjoy doing some of the work yourself, don't miss this special projects section. Here step-by-step photos and instructions will teach you how to install crown molding and wainscoting and how to tile a floor. You'll find easy decorative painting techniques, simple sewing projects, and super decorating ideas. Additional easy-to-create projects are also sprinkled throughout the book, making this the ultimate planning and do-it-yourself guide.

PLANNING GUIDE AND ARRANGING KIT

This important section takes you through the process of creating a budget for your new or remodeled bath and provides an easy-to-read chart to help you select bathroom components. Price ranges for surfaces, fixtures, and cabinetry are also provided. And when you are ready to start your bath makeover, the planning kit will help you design your dream bath—before enlisting the help of a professional.

CREDITS AND RESOURCES

This section provides designer contact information and resource listings for many of the products shown in the featured baths. A comprehensive index follows to help you quickly find specific topics.

Whether you are building a new home and seek inspiration for your bath or you are remodeling or redecorating an existing space, *HGTV Baths* is your all-in-one resource for expert advice, ideas, and planning strategies to create the right room for the way you live.

Every bathroom in this book is real, along with the design choices and decisions common to many homes. This is a book you will turn to again and again for practical advice and a plethora of information to make your bath the perfect fit for your family.

PAGE 53

PAGE 143

PAGE 60

From laying out a hardworking plan to choosing the best surfaces and fixtures to complement your bath and lifestyle, *HGTV Baths* has your bath decisions covered. Turn the page to begin an armchair tour of some of HGTV's most inspiring baths.

A **BATH** FOR EVERY **NEED**

Designing a bathroom that functions specifically for your needs is really about creating comfort—one of the single most important goals for your new space. Why? A bathroom that isn't efficient robs you of the ease you deserve for getting ready in the morning and winding down in the evening. The bathrooms and strategies in this section offer ideas to provide comfort for particular lifestyles and situations. Whether you are remodeling, adding on, or building a new home, you'll find solutions you can use to develop a functional plan.

SHOWER AMBITIONS

Tailor your master bathroom to meet your needs by choosing the amenities you'll use most.

Cabinetry fashioned from clear maple—a wood with subtle graining—forms the long dual-sink vanity and ensures the bathroom appears clean-lined and bright. Drawers and cabinets provide ample storage for two people.

To see how this same sleek style and smart storage work on a smaller scale, see the guest bath in this same house on page 20.

AN OVERSIZE JETTED BATHTUB remains a popular item to include in a bathroom, suggesting this must be an often-used amenity. But survey results tell a different story: Most people say they enjoy the experience but often don't take time to soak. If this sounds familiar, invest your space and budget in a design that skips the tub—but not the luxury—and centers around a well-appointed shower instead, similar to this spalike retreat.

SHOWER TIME

Make a wish list of everything you want a shower to provide. Would you like a generous space with multiple showerheads—at least one jetted showerhead and another handheld for easy rinsing? How about a bench so you have a place to relax and enjoy the steam? Would you appreciate speakers inside the shower so you can start and end the day with your favorite tunes? (The ideas on pages 18–19 offer some additional possibilities.) In a functional yet luxurious new home, this roomy shower, shown on page 14, offers all that, plus a door that pivots out for easy cleaning and in so drips run harmlessly back into the shower. (If you're updating an existing shower, consider installing a new showerhead with multiple spray options, a waterproof CD player/radio, and a pivoting door.)

Next think about how to pamper yourself after showering. The towel warmer just outside this shower allows the owners to wrap themselves in warmth and softness—a particular treat when it's cold outside. Towel warmers such as this can be added to a new or existing bathroom. Place a bench nearby so you can sit down while toweling off. The bench in this bath, shown on page 17, is large enough for both owners to sit down together and relax or take off their shoes.

This bath boils luxury down to its finer points. Even the gooseneck chrome faucets *far right* forego frills to present an unfettered arch and sleekly designed handles, which extend from a single plumbing connection. An elegant granite countertop provides the most notable pattern.

Built-in storage *right* puts towels and toiletries in the bathroom where they're needed while providing a smooth look that suits this clean-lined bath.

Italian tile and polished chrome fixtures lend a luxurious spalike feel to this spacious walk-in shower in a master bathroom with no jetted tub (though the house does have an outdoor hot tub). A variety of showerheads offers showering options for two. Locating the towel warmer right outside the shower provides convenience and comfort.

VANITY FAIR

When it's time to get ready for the day or to wind down for bedtime, a nicely equipped vanity assures you won't stress after a relaxing shower. The long, clean-lined vanity in this bathroom offers two large undermount sinks equipped with tall, shiny chrome gooseneck faucets on a dark granite countertop. Drawers and cabinets store toiletries close at hand. The open shelves on the walls flanking the vanity provide a place for a clock, soaps, and treasures.

EASY DIVISION

When designing a bathroom around a walk-in shower, add compartment spaces off the central vanity area to increase storage and privacy. This bathroom offers a private toilet compartment with a door (not shown), a built-in storage unit with drawers and cabinets, and a closet large enough to serve as a dressing room (see floor plan *opposite above*). All these amenities fit into a relatively modest space—a design feat that wouldn't have been possible if an oversize jetted tub had been part of the plan.

For more shower ideas, see pages 18–19.

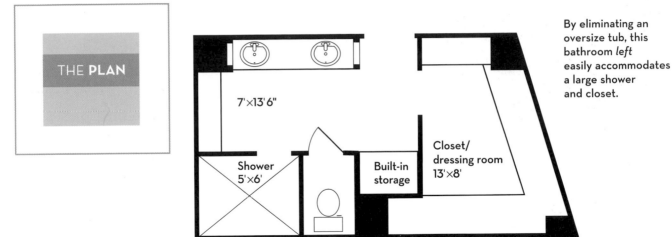

THE **PLAN**

7'×13'6"

Shower
5'×6'

Built-in
storage

Closet/
dressing room
13'×8'

By eliminating an
oversize tub, this
bathroom *left*
easily accommodates
a large shower
and closet.

TOWEL WARMERS

IMAGINE STEPPING out of the shower (or tub) and wrapping up in a warm
towel. Heated towel bars, used in this bath built by Haskins Design Group,
make it possible. Towel warmers come in two types: hydronic and electric.

HYDRONIC WARMERS circulate either hot water or steam through the
tubular brass on the rack and transfer heat to textiles lying on the surface.
Homes with boiler systems for central heating typically use hydronic racks.
These racks may also be installed by tapping into an existing hot-water tank
in a home or by installing a miniature portable water heater dedicated to
serving a towel warmer. Valves control the warmers, "mixing" cold and hot
water to achieve the desired temperature.

ELECTRIC WARMERS circulate a light oil (much like mineral oil) within the
tubing; an electric rod heats the oil similar to the way electric water heaters
perform. Hydronic units are usually less expensive to operate and heat more
quickly than electric ones, which typically take 15 to 60 minutes to warm
up. Most people install a programmable timer on the electric towel warmer,
so they're greeted with warm towels when they step out of the shower.

TYPICAL COSTS for either kind of towel-warming unit depend on the size,
type of finish, and any customization. Good-quality units start at $300 to
$800 and can run up to $2,000 to $3,000 or well beyond.

Capturing space within walls flanking the vanity *above* provides a place for the owners to display personal belongings.

On the window wall between the shower and vanity, this long bench provides a place to relax after a shower. Baskets slipped beneath the bench offer storage for towels.

SHOWER SAVVY

Great showers and shower systems, like the one shown on pages 12–17, begin with the showerheads and wrap up with the stall configurations. Here's a look at some of the options.

PARTIAL ENCLOSURE In a smaller bathroom consider a shower with a partial glass enclosure to reflect the spray back into the stall; the open entry keeps the look clean. Mismatched dual showerheads offer two spray options. This shower *below* also features a tiled bench and storage ledges beside each showerhead.

EASY ENTRANCE Design a shower without a door or a threshold for easy access and easier cleaning. A shower entrance without a raised threshold allows a wheelchair to maneuver inside. This shower *above* is roomy enough for two and features a teak bench for relaxing and a built-in niche on the sidewall for shampoo, soap, and accessories.

PAMPERING POINTERS

GREAT SHOWERHEADS depend on two things: the range of coverage (how much of your skin the water hits) and the design of the spray heads (the pattern of the water flow). Don't be fooled into thinking that the more holes there are in a showerhead face, the more coverage you get. The art of a showerhead is in well-planned, full-coverage water-spray patterns.

INEXPENSIVE PLASTIC SHOWERHEADS and handheld shower wands available at home centers offer some form of multiple spray patterns. The most expensive fixed showerheads can have 10 settings or more. Common spray patterns include a wide spray, a soft spray (an aerated spray), a stinging-needle jet spray, and a massage spray. Some luxury showers include a waterfall feature, such as the one shown on page 61.

SHOWERS today typically combine a number of showerheads and body sprays. Body sprays attach to the shower wall usually about 12 to 24 inches from where the user stands. When installing side sprays, plan for a larger water heater that holds at least 50 to 75 gallons.

PRICES FOR SHOWERHEADS can range from less than $10 to more than $100. Most people spend $30 to $40 for a "luxury" model. Custom shower systems featuring waterfalls, multiple showerheads, body sprays, temperature-control gauges, and sound cost as much as $10,000.

TOTALLY SEALED This shower *above*, though tightly enclosed for steaming, feels bright and open, thanks to the clear glass door and windows and an interior glass ceiling with skylights. Dual showerheads feature separate controls, allowing a couple to share the shower. The 6-foot-long bench invites sitting or stretching out while steaming.

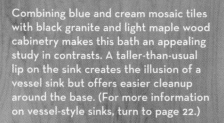

Combining blue and cream mosaic tiles with black granite and light maple wood cabinetry makes this bath an appealing study in contrasts. A taller-than-usual lip on the sink creates the illusion of a vessel sink but offers easier cleanup around the base. (For more information on vessel-style sinks, turn to page 22.)

FINEST SECOND

Your second bath needn't be second best. This bathroom shows you can have function and beauty.

Suspending the vanity base between the tall storage counters so it appears to hover above the floor makes this element *right* appear lighter so it doesn't overpower the small room. Lighting beneath the countertop edge is as practical as it is beautiful, providing a subtle glow at nighttime.

ALTHOUGH A SECOND BATH often features modest dimensions, your family and visitors can enjoy similar convenience, beauty, and luxury typically reserved for a large master bathroom. Let this second-to-none bath (located in the same house as the master bathroom on page 12) help guide your planning.

CENTRAL STATION

For a second bathroom to be useful, locate it between popular congregating spots in your house and the bedroom or bedrooms it will serve. Conveniently located beside a kitchen and family room, this full bathroom takes the place of a powder room. Equipped with a shower and bathtub combination, this bath also accommodates a "flex room," a space designed to perform as an office and/or as a bedroom.

VERTICAL STORAGE

Whether your second bathroom will serve overnight guests or family members,

include as much storage as possible in this typical 5×7-foot or 5×8-foot space. Flanking the sink vanity in this bathroom, vertical cabinets stack up a surprising amount of storage from floor to ceiling (see page 23). Although the dual tower storage limits the amount of counter space around the sink, there is plenty of space for soap and accessories. The towers keep clutter out of sight. (In an existing bathroom, you could increase storage by constructing one or two cabinet towers on the countertop.)

Also consider an additional built-in storage unit in lieu of a standard linen closet. This bathroom features a built-in unit of drawers and doors, eliminating the inconvenience of a large closet door swinging into the small space. A pair of extra-deep drawers (see page 22) is ideal for storing bulky items, such as a hair dryer or an electric foot bath. Including deep drawers and adjustable shelves in cabinets allows the flexibility required for

Cabinetry in clear maple, which is subtly grained, and simple silvery knobs *above* continue the clean, contemporary look of the bathroom.

VESSEL SINKS

IN THE QUEST FOR STYLE, vessel sinks, which look like a bowl sitting on (see page 142) or partially below (see *opposite* and page 54) the counter, are gaining popularity. Here are some factors you'll need to consider when including one in your plans:

FAUCET HEIGHT. Standard bathroom faucets won't accommodate the taller basins, which typically stand at least 5 inches above the counter—and often much higher. Use a wall-mounted or a gooseneck faucet. If you decide on a wall-mounted faucet, plumbing for the faucet will need to be installed before the drywall.

DRAIN STOPPERS. A bar faucet is an acceptable and workable solution to the tall-faucet dilemma. Keep in mind that drain releases usually aren't available with nonbath fittings, so you may need to purchase a rubber stopper or a pop-up manual drain. In a guest bathroom where the bowl may not need to hold water, use a simple wire grid over the drain.

AMOUNT OF USE. Take care in deciding what kind of use a bath gets before opting for an easily breakable water-vessel sink. Something as small as a dropped perfume bottle easily could chip or crack a vessel sink made from glass or pottery.

SPLASH POTENTIAL. Some above-counter sinks are very shallow. A faucet set too high above a shallow sink can result in a lot of water splashing out, requiring frequent cleanups.

USER HEIGHT. Consider the height of the people who will use the basin and the height of the vessel bowl, then adjust the cabinet height accordingly for optimum comfort.

Porcelain tiles on the floor and bathtub surround look like stone but offer the imperviousness of a ceramic finish *opposite*. Designer and master builder Ralph Haskins keeps grout lines between tiles at 3/16 inch to keep the look clean and to minimize maintenance.

storing discount club items—a bonus if you stock up in bulk.

LIGHT SIDE

In a small bathroom selecting light-color finishes prevents the space from feeling closed in. White fixtures, a white shower curtain, and a bathtub surround and flooring in stonelike Italian porcelain tiles make this modestly sized bathroom feel larger than its true dimensions.

Suspending the vanity between the storage towers—rather than setting the vanity cabinet on the floor—enhances the sense of spaciousness in the room as well. The cabinet doors on the towers are translucent because extra-tall, solid cabinet doors would have overwhelmed the space. The degree of opaqueness creates the sense of something beyond the door without revealing the contents of the cabinet interiors.

For more information on smart storage solutions for a bath, turn the page.

A round mirror and vessel-like sink *below* introduce some eye-pleasing curves to balance the crisp, straight lines of the tiles, granite countertop, and flanking cabinetry.

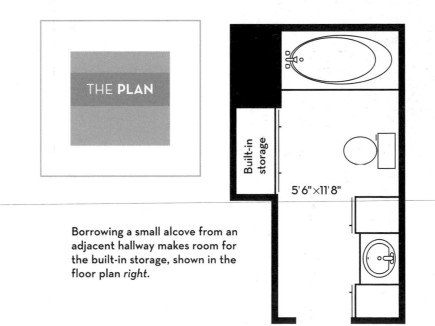

THE **PLAN**

Built-in storage

5'6"×11'8"

Borrowing a small alcove from an adjacent hallway makes room for the built-in storage, shown in the floor plan *right*.

SMART STORAGE STRATEGIES

Make every inch count in your bathroom—large or small, as the one on pages 20-23 demonstrates— with smart storage solutions like these.

PULLOUT STORAGE Dead space between cabinets can go to work as additional storage. This pullout *left* stores a surprising number of lotions and other toiletries, becoming practically invisible when closed.

SLIM STORAGE Transform a decorative sink vanity panel into tilt-out storage, such as the example shown *right*. New cabinets often offer similar built-in features. Or use a kit complete with hinges and a bin to modify an existing vanity. Include a hidden electrical outlet for extra convenience. Make sure the outlets in your bath are ground fault circuit interrupted for safety.

HIDDEN HAMPER A door reveals a slide-out hamper *above*. Look for built-in hamper designs that allow you to easily remove the hamper—whether wire, plastic, or fabric—and tote it to your washer and dryer.

ADDED ASSETS A window seat located just above baseboard heat offers towel bins with drop-down doors *right*. With the bins directly above the heat, towels come out toasty warm on cold days.

NIFTY NICHE Keep storage out in the open to encourage children to hang up towels and put away toys. This tiled niche *above* features pegs for towels, a bench for storing togs or sitting down, and a wire toy basket that slips beneath the bench.

A pair of glass walls makes the 4-foot-square shower seem even more spacious. A wide ledge between the shower and tub provides storage and display space for towels and candles.

CLEAN GETAWAY

Designed as a tranquil yet functional master retreat, this bath features easy-care surfaces and pampering amenities.

Creamy travertine countertops *above right* reflect plenty of natural and artificial light, making shaving and applying makeup easier on the eyes. Single-lever faucets complement the streamlined look and enable the owners to turn the water on and off with a flick of the wrist.

A pair of built-in niches—one shown *below right* and both shown *opposite*—provides handy storage for soaps. A massaging showerhead reduces tension as you wash.

"SIMPLIFY YOUR LIFE" is the mantra for many people, and this well-planned bath makes morning and night cleanup rituals efficient and stress-free. To create similar functionality in your bath, choose a hardworking layout, easy-care surfaces, and effective lighting. Read on to learn how to incorporate this design into your lifestyle.

PRIVATE SPACES

If you have plenty of square footage as this bath does (see the floor plan on page 28), include separate vanities so you and your mate can have personalized storage and grooming space. This pentagon-shaped bath features two 10-foot-long vanities that run perpendicular to one another and meet in a corner. Sinks placed near the opposite ends of each vanity provide ample elbow room between each user. The extra-long cream-color stone vanities provide storage for toiletries, hair dryers, and towels, alleviating the need for a separate linen closet. The extra counter space near the vertex of the counter serves as a convenient makeup center.

Separating the shower and tub increases efficiency; both fixtures can be used at the same time when the owners are pressed for time. Plus, on days when both owners choose to shower or bathe, they save time cleaning only one fixture. A separate toilet area (not shown) ensures privacy.

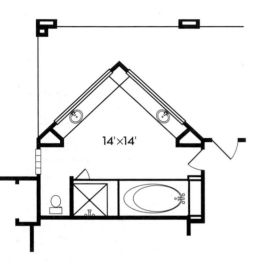

14'×14'

This unusually shaped bath *above* takes advantage of exterior wall space with three windows—two above the vanities and one between the vanity and toilet compartment. Ample floor space between the vanities and shower/tub wall makes the bath feel spacious and luxurious. The area could also easily accommodate a chaise longue or a pair of cushy upholstered chairs.

Form and function unite in this ageless bath, designed by architect and builder Phillip Vlieger. A pair of extra-long vanities made from warm cherry wood *right* provides enough storage for a couple and even a child or visitor.

SURFACE SOLUTIONS

To reduce cleanup chores choose surfaces that disguise water spots and resist lime and soap buildup. Here two shades of natural travertine line the shower and cover the floor. The stone rinses clean with little or no scrubbing thanks to its ultrasmooth surface. The mottled pattern of the stone also disguises water spots and footprints. Fuss-free lightly stained cherry wood cabinets feature a matte polyurethane finish that can be wiped clean with a dustcloth; storage organizers inside the drawers and pullout shelves inside the cabinets keep supplies organized and within easy reach.

FIRE AND LIGHT

To warm the bath during the cooler months and provide a relaxing kinetic glow whatever the season, install a double-sided fireplace for use in both the master bedroom and the master bath as shown *opposite.* Maximize natural light in the bath by including as many windows as possible. Sunlight is great for applying makeup for daytime events, and it is a natural spirit lifter. In this bath a floor-to-ceiling glass-block window at

the left end of one vanity and clerestory windows positioned on the bulkhead above the mirror on each vanity flood the room with daylight each morning without sacrificing privacy. A trio of recessed fixtures above each vanity enhances natural light as necessary. Recessed fixtures designed for wet areas illuminate the tub and shower.

For more information on proper bath lighting, turn the page.

Two shades of travertine tiles connect the tub, shower, and fireplace surround, creating a stunning focal point. The whirlpool tub is roomy enough for two. Clean-lined fixtures match the ones chosen for the sinks and include a handheld spray.

THE RIGHT LIGHT

As the bath on pages 26–29 illustrates, proper lighting provides shadowless, glare-free illumination throughout a room and makes applying makeup and shaving easier on the eye.

AMBIENT AND TASK Ambient lighting creates a uniform, overall glow in the bath space. This type of light comes from one or more, usually overhead, sources. (If your bath is larger than 35 square feet, one overhead fixture will not be enough.) Supplement general lighting with task lighting. Position these fixtures to eliminate shadows in the areas where you perform specific tasks such as applying makeup, shaving, or taking a bath.

LIGHTING THE MIRROR Because the bathroom mirror often serves as the primary grooming center, ensure proper lighting by placing fixtures so the light distributes evenly from all sides of the mirror. This crosslighting prevents shadows, which can make applying makeup difficult. You can create crosslighting by combining downlights and sconces with a white countertop as shown in this bath *above*. The white countertop reflects light from below up onto the face, enhancing the lighting quality.

LIGHTING THE SHOWER AND TUB In an enclosed shower or tub compartment, most building codes require vapor-proof fixtures. Place the fixtures so they fully light the area but don't shine in your eyes when you're relaxing in the tub. All light switches should be at least 6 feet from the water source to reduce the risk of electrocution.

VANITY BULBS

CHOOSE BULBS designed for vanity illumination; these bulbs create light in the daylight spectrum range. Do not choose bulbs that are too white or too yellow, because the mirror won't reflect a true picture of how you look outside the bathroom.

INCANDESCENT. Introduced by Thomas Edison in 1879, incandescent bulbs are still widely used and appreciated for the light they offer. More energy-efficient, longer-lasting incandescent bulbs are available today. Low-voltage incandescent fixtures make good accent lighting.

FLUORESCENT. Fluorescent tubes are energy efficient and last far longer than incandescent bulbs. Today's tubes reduce the noise and flicker associated with earlier models and come in a wide spectrum of colors. New subcompact tubes can be used in fixtures that usually require incandescent bulbs.

HALOGEN. Quartz halogen lights offer bright light that's good for task or accent lighting. Usually low voltage, these bulbs put out a large amount of heat, so they should be used only in fixtures designed for halogen bulbs.

NIGHT-LIGHTS Night-lights make nighttime trips to the bathroom more comfortable. For an easy, affordable solution, plug in an automatic night-light that senses the amount of light coming into the room. Or install rope lights below the vanity toe-kick or above wall cabinets to provide soft illumination. In the bath *right* and on pages 66–69 the owner installed a bulb socket inside the vanity bases. When on, the light shines through the translucent glass sink, creating a beautiful night-light.

When time permits a whirlpool tub relaxes sore muscles. A glass-block window behind the tub provides privacy from a neighboring house while allowing in ample sunlight. The bath "rug" is made from slip-proof ceramic tile, making cleanup easy and safety a priority. The door to the left of the tub (out of view) leads to "his" closet; the door on the right connects to the private shower and toilet area.

PERSONAL PLAN

If you plan your bath to match your lifestyle, you can save time and reduce stress.

IF YOU ARE TIRED OF DANCING around your mate or your children as you shuffle between the sink and the shower, design a bath to match your family's needs. The more precisely you define your needs and priorities before building or remodeling, the more likely the final design will meet your expectations. (For help determining your bath goals, see "Capturing Your Dreams" on page 34.)

After sharing tract-home baths for more than 20 years, the owners of this bath had a clear picture of what they wanted from the space. They selected decorative, slip-resistant tiles and a seamless solid-surfacing sink and counter combination for lasting style and ease of care. Separate vanities, separate closets, a private shower and toilet area, and easy access to a laundry area were all priorities. (See the floor plan on page 34.) Read on to find out how you can adapt this floor plan to create a bath that works for your situation.

VANITY SMARTS

Whether you choose to share a vanity or build separate ones, the area should provide enough storage and counter space for everyone who uses it. To maximize storage in this bath, the owners chose kitchen cabinets for the vanity bases instead of bath cabinets. Taller and deeper than standard vanity cabinets (vanity cabinets typically measure 30 inches high and 18 to 21 inches deep), the tall owners find the 36-inch counter height more comfortable. They also appreciate the extra storage the added depth (kitchen cabinets are typically 36 inches deep) and taller height provide.

COMPARTMENTALIZED PLAN

Separate closet areas double as dressing rooms. As the plan on page 34 shows, "her" closet is large enough to store everything from undergarments and shoes to off-season clothing. Although "his" closet is smaller, dressing in the space is still possible, and storage drawers and shelves organize undergarments, socks, and shoes. A combined toilet and shower compartment to the right of the tub enables the vanity area and closets to be accessible to other family members without sacrificing privacy.

GOOD CONNECTIONS

Often overlooked in bath planning, connecting the bath to other areas can increase convenience. The owners opted to join the bath to the laundry area, so towels and dirty clothes can be transferred easily to the laundry. The laundry also connects to a home office, making it easier for the owners to tend to the laundry during breaks in the workday. For more information on selecting a floor plan that will work best for you and your family, see page 36.

You don't have to be an experienced carpenter to create a tub apron like this one. Although the raised panels *above* look custom, they are actually three ready-made cabinet doors attached to a painted and polyurethane-coated plywood base. One door opens to provide access to the tub plumbing.

PAINTING STRIPES

WALL STRIPES of varying widths, as shown *below*, are soft, subtle, and easy to create. First paint the walls with a base coat of a light color; let the base coat dry. Starting at one corner use white chalk to measure and mark the walls at 8-, 12-, and 14-inch increments. Use a carpenter's level and the chalk to make floor-to-ceiling dotted lines at the measured increments. Then mask off the marked lines with low-tack painter's tape. Fill in alternate stripes with a darker shade of paint. While the paint is still wet, carefully remove the painter's tape; let the paint dry.

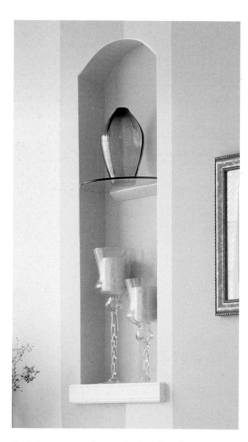

A niche recessed into the stud wall separating the bath from the private toilet and shower compartment *above* provides storage and display space for decorative accessories.

CAPTURING YOUR DREAMS

TO DETERMINE what you want most from your bath, ask yourself the following questions. Your answers will provide you with a list of amenities that will make your bath a better fit for your family.

DO YOU NEED to share the bath regularly with another person? If so what amenities, such as two sinks or a private toilet area, would make sharing the bath more convenient and more comfortable?

DO YOU USE a bathtub on a regular basis or could the space be better utilized by another amenity, such as a storage armoire as shown on page 128, a makeup center as shown on page 80, or a steam shower for two as shown on page 18?

IF YOU ARE PLANNING a bath just for kids, how could a new layout enable two or more kids to comfortably utilize the space at the same time? (See the Jack-and-Jill bath layouts on page 37 for ideas.)

IS THE ROOM USED primarily for showering or does it also serve as a place to apply makeup, shave, and get dressed?

DOES THE BATHROOM relate to adjacent rooms the way you would like it to? The bath shown connects to a laundry to save the owners steps while transferring towels and clothing to and from each area.

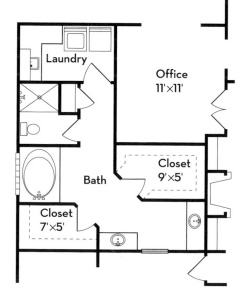

Laundry

Office
11'×11'

Bath

Closet
9'×5'

Closet
7'×5'

A hardworking layout *left* makes this bath the perfect complement to a working couple's active life. His-and-her vanities, his-and-her closets, and an enclosed private shower and toilet area make the vanities and closets accessible while still providing privacy for someone using the shower or toilet. A connection to the laundry room reduces the steps required to transfer clean and dirty clothes and linens between closets and machines. By connecting the laundry area to the home office, whoever is working from home can keep the washing machine humming as the workday progresses.

THE PLAN

Banks of drawers in the vanity base provide storage for makeup, hair supplies, toiletries, and cleaning products. Narrow shelves next to the vanity hold additional toiletries and display artwork. A standard kitchen appliance garage conceals curling irons and hair dryers. Instead of choosing clear glass for the flanking wall cabinets, the owners opted for mirrors that hide cabinet contents.

HARDWORKING PLANS

The bath featured on pages 32–35 was designed to match the owners' individual needs. To make your bath a better fit for your lifestyle, put one of these bath plans to work in your home.

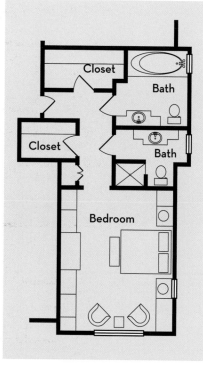

TWO BATHS If you've never savored the thought of sharing bath space with a guest or even a spouse, build two smaller baths in the same amount of space usually occupied by a single bath, as shown *above*. The configuration also works well in homes where a guest room and child's room are adjacent to one another.

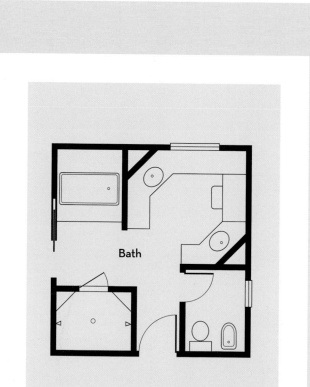

COMPARTMENTALIZED MASTER In this plan a private compartment houses a toilet and a bidet. A curtain sections off the tub and a door with frosted glass provides privacy in the shower. The vanity area divides into two sections, one for him and one for her.

OUTDOOR ACCESS Although baths are often on outside walls, rarely is that proximity to the outdoors used to an advantage. This bath *below* connects to a private patio. Within the bath glass-block walls allow light to filter into the private toilet compartment and the shower.

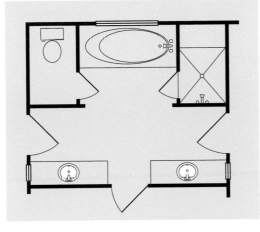

THESE COMPARTMENTALIZED baths feature separate vanity areas and tub/shower/toilet closets. These plans are particularly popular for baths shared by siblings or by a child's room and a guest bedroom. The plans are often referred to as Jack-and-Jill layouts.

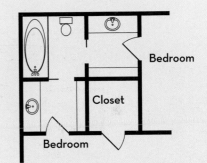

Bedroom

Closet

Bedroom

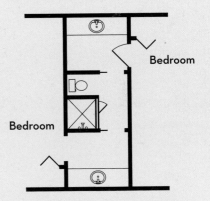

Bedroom

Bedroom

BATH FOR TWO Designed for two family members to use simultaneously, this bath *left* features an interior pocket door to create privacy within a limited amount of space. Adding a second pocket door to the wall across from the sinks could create access to another bedroom, hallway, or closet.

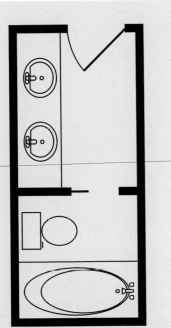

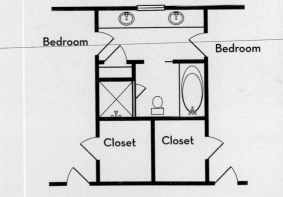

Bedroom

Bedroom

Closet

Closet

The only hints that this bath and the one in the Before photo *opposite below left* are one and the same are the locations of the fixtures and the window. Updated fixtures, surface upgrades, and fresh paint make the space look like new.

SAME-SPACE SOLUTIONS

Update your present bath with new fixtures and surfaces that will look great now and in the future.

YOU DON'T HAVE to expand the size of your bath or change the placement of fixtures to make the room more attractive and functional. In this bath all the fixtures remain in the same places to keep plumbing costs in check, while the upgrades in quality and style make the room feel and live larger.

PAINTED STYLE

If your existing cabinetry is structurally sound, update it with a fresh coat of paint; for more warmth and visual depth coat the new finish with glaze or stain. Here the original white-painted vanity base was retained but bumped out 2 inches to allow enough space for two larger sinks. New knobs and handles add style and texture. You can also enliven the walls with a cheerful paint color. In this bath deep blue walls allow the crisp white cabinets to take center stage.

Before the remodel dated wallpaper and worn fixtures made this bath look tired *left*. Today new surfaces and fixtures make the room stylish and inviting.

The vanity cabinet *top* and the large window *above* are the only holdovers from the original bath. New paint, knobs, and handles make the vanity look as fresh as the rest of the bath. A new valance and a top-lowering pleated shade update the window and provide privacy.

Under-the-shelf wire storage baskets *above left* put often-wasted space to work and alleviate the need for lots of stacking. The wire baskets, available at home centers and discount stores, can be retrofitted into existing cabinets.

Neatness is easy in a bath equipped with accessible storage. Pullout baskets *above center* hold a variety of bath supplies. These wicker baskets and metal tracks are also available at home centers and can be installed in existing cabinets.

Crown molding tops each of the new bookcases: two units have solid doors, and one includes a pair of glass doors to create an attractive storage center *above right*.

NO WASTED SPACE

Gain more storage by filling empty walls with bookcases or open shelves; then maximize the capacity of each cabinet with organizers that put every inch of space to use. The owners of this bath purchased traditional-style unfinished bookcases and topped them with crown molding *opposite right* for a built-in appearance. Fresh paint and matching hardware finish the bookcases and visually tie them to the vanity base. Pullout baskets and stacking shelves organize supplies. A new larger soaking tub takes up less space than a worn freestanding model that extended into the traffic path. Two large rectangular sinks contain splashes better than the original models.

Durable stone-look engineered quartz replaces aging laminate counters. Easy-care, tumbled-stone tiles make up a new tub surround and replace the tattered vinyl floor. For more information on selecting flooring for your bath, turn to page 44.

To bring more style, color, and organization into your bath use painted wicker baskets adorned with fabric liners to hold less attractive fare, such as hair ties and styling brushes. Display stacked towels in complementary colors and relegate the faded ones to the garage. Show off soaps and bath salts in pretty containers. Painted baskets and wire half-shelves *above,* keep bath accessories in the glass-fronted bookcase looking neat and attractive.

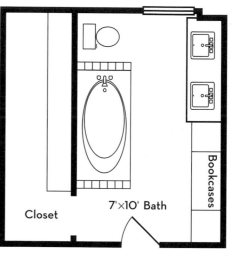

Bookcases

Closet   7'×10' Bath

A trio of bookcases fills once-empty wall space and triples the amount of storage *above*. A new apron-front tub replaces the old claw-foot model.

A new massaging shower spray *opposite top* takes the sting out of giving up a whirlpool tub (see "Remodeling Reality" *opposite right*). The adjustable head moves up and down to accommodate the different heights of the owners.

A recessed niche in the shower surround *opposite center* holds soap and shampoos. A pinwheel pattern of 1×2-inch stone tiles adds interest to the walls.

A glass-block partition *opposite bottom* separates the new tub from the closet entrance and prevents the narrow passage from feeling confining.

Glass blocks above the showerhead allow light to flow from the toilet compartment into the tub area *above*. A handmade shower curtain softens the hard lines of the stone tile and brings more color and pattern into the room.

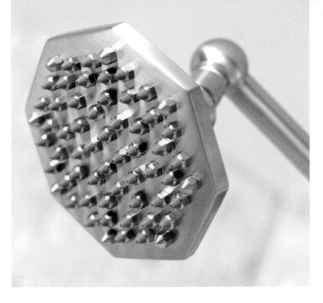

REMODELING REALITY

PLAN FOR SURPRISES and compromises when remodeling any room of your home. Unanticipated findings, such as faulty wiring or deteriorating pipes—especially if your home is older— may come to light during construction. These problems may adversely affect the price or the outcome of your project. Although the owners of this bath planned to upgrade to a whirlpool tub, the new wiring required for the motor made the change cost prohibitive, so the couple opted for a soaking tub. The wrong size of soaking tub was delivered to the home twice, and the third tub delivered was damaged—adding stress and time delays to the project. Despite these remodeling pitfalls, the owners got everything else they wanted and are pleased with the outcome of the project. View inevitable changes like these with a positive attitude and enjoy the challenge of finding a workable solution. In the end your beautiful new bathroom will only add to the enjoyment—and likely the value—of your home.

Engineered quartz tops the vanity and serves as a backsplash *right*. The undermount sinks eliminate crevices and make cleaning easier. Nickel-color paint gives the brass-framed mirror a decorative lift.

FLOOR SHOW

The bathroom on pages 38–43 benefited from updated flooring. Look here to find the flooring material with the right style and function for your bath.

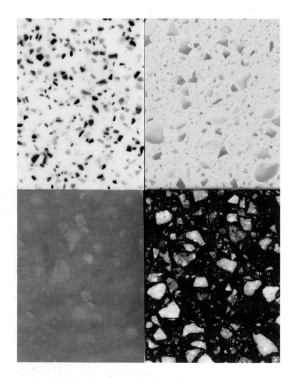

ENGINEERED QUARTZ Engineered quartz *above* can be used on floors and counters and mimics the function of natural stone. It costs about the same as granite but offers a wider range of colors.

TILE Whether ceramic, porcelain, or natural stone, tile makes an excellent flooring choice in a bath because it stands up to traffic, hair spray, lotions, and moisture. For extra opulence without breaking the budget, install heating coils below the surface to keep your toes warm and toasty when you're barefoot in the bath. The natural stone tiles *below* (from the bathroom featured on pages 78–83) create an attractive flooring surface that's easy to clean and naturally slip resistant.

BAMBOO From Asian forests to your bath, bamboo is the "hardwood" of choice among environmentally conscious buyers. As durable underfoot as most tree-grown woods, bamboo grass grows much faster, making it a renewable resource.

LAMINATE Durable and easy-to-clean laminate *below* makes an excellent flooring choice for the bath. Water-resistant laminate stands up to moisture better than most natural woods and is available in wood, stone, and tile motifs. Note that not all laminate brands are recommended for "wet" areas, so review the manufacturer's literature before selecting the brand for your bath.

VINYL Resilient vinyl *above* feels soft underfoot and can be installed over other hard, flat surfaces in a few hours. A wide selection of colors and styles, including stone, tile, and hardwood look-alikes, makes this affordably priced material a good choice for any bath requiring a quick fix.

LESS
IS MORE

Make the most of the square footage you have in and around your bath with an efficient, amenity-packed layout.

Because this relatively small bath is packed with function, the architect kept the overall design simple so the bath would feel open and inviting, not cramped. Smooth-front custom cabinets *opposite* are made from sheets of inexpensive birch plywood. To ensure the wood grains match, each piece of plywood was hand selected, with consecutive drawers made from the same sheet. The vanity counter, made of shiny black granite, provides interesting contrast against the white porcelain undermount sinks. Mounted on the mirror, three-bulb sconces create excellent illumination.

IF PLUMBING LINES, chimney flues, or load-bearing walls limit your access to floor space, there are other ways to make a small bath look, feel, and live larger.

GRAND ILLUSIONS

Wrapping materials from one surface to another and choosing light- and bright-color or shiny, reflective materials create illusions of spaciousness. In this 100-square-foot bath, 2-inch-square ceramic tiles connect the floor to the walls, making the change of planes less noticeable. The small tile pattern also makes the narrow trafficway seem wider. A counter-to-ceiling mirror covers the wall behind the vanity, another space-expanding strategy. Bright blue-color reflective glass tiles line the shower walls opposite the vanity; insets of glass accent tiles in other vivid colors add whimsy. Pure white 6-inch-square ceramic tiles connect the white tub surround to the adjacent wall.

A LITTLE SOMETHING EXTRA

If possible look to adjacent rooms when remodeling to gain slivers of floor space that can provide room for an amenity you

Before the remodel this bath *below* was uncomfortable for even one person, offering little natural light and no counter space.

BEFORE

A wide ledge behind the tub *top* provides storage and display for artwork and necessities.

To make drawer stacks line up, the architect designed the drawers near the sink to have partially false fronts *above*. Although smaller than they appear from the outside, the drawers still provide a significant amount of storage.

47

The gray-tiled tub deck extends into the shower to provide a seat *right*. On the tub side, the deck holds spare towels, toiletries, and a collection of funky artwork. Glass shower walls also heighten the illusion of spaciousness. Random rectangles of brightly colored accent tiles create a playful ambience. A 6-inch tile lip keeps shower water from spilling into the walkway.

always wanted. To gain floor space in this bath, the owners bumped the vanity wall 2 feet into an adjacent master bedroom and a connecting hall. A new 7½-foot-long custom vanity fills the niche gained from the master bedroom and offers eight drawers for each user as well as storage beneath each sink base. A pair of medicine cabinets recessed into tile-covered walls also provides storage near each sink.

Space borrowed from the hall provides room for a separate air-jet tub *opposite* (a must-have for one of the owners), a separate shower with a seat, and a private toilet compartment shown on page 50. (For more ways to gain floor space see "Exploring Space" on page 57. For information on air-jet tubs, see "Tub Talk" on page 59.)

If your bath is located on an exterior wall as this one is, add more windows or increase the size of the existing ones. Windows let in natural light, fresh air, and scenic views, preventing small rooms from feeling cramped. Although the window in this bath remains in its original spot, a black granite-top ledge, white-painted woodwork, and white mullions

GLASS TILE

AN INCREASINGLY popular surfacing choice, translucent architectural glass tiles sparkle in the sunlight and bring a sense of depth and color to a wall or counter. More durable than glass panes, the material works well for walls, backsplashes, and countertops, but it is not recommended for floors. The tiles can also be backlit to bring more sparkle to a room. (For more surfacing options, see pages 44-45 and pages 96-97.)

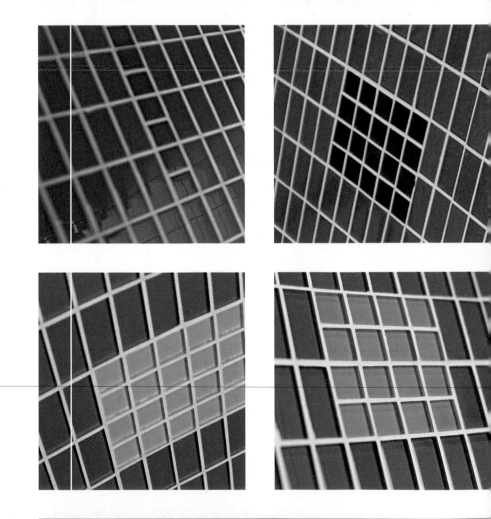

ART IN THE BATH

MAKE YOUR bath feel more personal and inviting by hanging framed art as shown *below* and displaying vases or hand-carved sculptures as shown on the window ledge on page 48. Choose pieces that won't be damaged by heat or humidity, such as glazed ceramics and glass-enclosed prints.

THE **PLAN**

To prevent the toilet compartment from looking like everybody else's, a custom piece of art hangs behind the commode *above*.

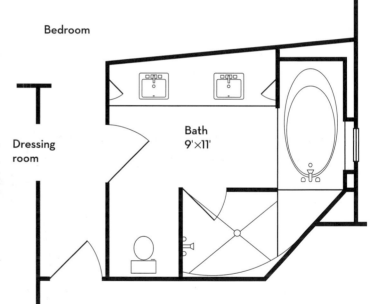

Bedroom

Dressing room

Bath
9'×11'

Slivers of space gained from adjoining areas make this bath accommodating for two. When added to the existing area, the extra square footage provides room for an air-jet tub, a separate shower, a double vanity with two sinks, and a private toilet compartment.

draw more attention to it and the wooded view beyond. The new ledge matches the granite vanity top and also provides storage and display space.

THE ROOM NEXT DOOR

To reduce the amount of time each person needs to spend in the bath, look for ways to increase the functionality of the rooms. Place a sink in a bedroom storage chest so you don't have to be in the bath to wash your hands and face or brush your teeth. If a makeup counter is more important to you than a second sink, replace a basic dresser with a vanity table complete with storage drawers and a lighted mirror. Or if a spare bedroom is only a few steps from your master bath, turn it into a spacious dressing room. The dressing room shown on pages 52–53 was once a rarely used spare room located just across the hall from this bath. To learn more about laying out a dressing room of your own, turn the page.

To make the shower *above* as safe and comfortable as possible, the owners included a sturdy grab bar and a shaving mirror. The adjustable showerhead offers a pulsating water massage.

ROOM FOR DRESSING

A separate dressing area takes the pressure off the bedroom and the bath by increasing closet space and providing a place to dress. This dream closet is located just across the hall from the bath on pages 46–51.

SAVVY STORAGE This functional dressing area *above* was once a spare bedroom. Now hanging rods, storage drawers, and open cubbies line the walls of the room. High storage holds less-frequently used items and stays neat with large wicker baskets.

DRESS FOR SUCCESS Make the room even more useful by including a pullout ironing board and a folding area. In this dressing room a center island provides drawer-filled space for folding and packing clothes. On the end of the island closest to the window, a conveniently located pullout ironing board *below* minimizes steps to a freestanding clothes rack.

ASSESSING YOUR NEEDS

TO TRANSFORM your spare room into a dressing mecca, first assess your current storage needs. Do you wear everything that's stashed in your existing closet? If not remove what you never wear and donate it to charity or sell it at a yard sale. Then measure how much hanging, drawer, and shelf storage you feel is necessary to make everything neat and tidy, but not crowded. Look for closet organizers to keep things uncluttered. Include space for lingerie, socks, garments, and accessories.

WHICH SHOE IS WHICH?

Trying to remember what is stored in which basket or box can be difficult. To eliminate the problem label and attach key tags, available at office supply stores, or glue computer-printed labels to basket fronts. In this closet each shoebox *left* sports a digital photo of the box's contents.

REUSE, RECYCLE To cut down on cabinetry and shelving costs, recycle drawers and shelves from other remodeled spaces in your home. These drawers *left* came from the original bath and a nearby linen closet. The cubbies to the right of the drawers are new and keep shoes and bags neat and readily accessible. To make the closet feel welcoming, artwork and accessories decorate a few of the shelves as shown *left* and *opposite far left*.

53

Honed-slate countertops combine with maple cabinetry to offer eye-pleasing contrast with the shining finishes of the porcelain sink and the chrome faucet.

BROADER BOUNDARIES

If your bathroom territory seems as cramped as this space once was, it may be time to expand beyond the borders.

BEFORE A MAKEOVER by *Designers' Challenge* chosen designer Linda Maglia, this dark bathroom featured a long vanity squeezed into a narrow hall-like entry area. Although the shower was fairly nice, the homeowner didn't care for the shallow bathtub and wished instead for a deep soaking tub. One of the more promising existing design features in the room was an atrium window where the homeowner envisioned a Zenlike view with rocks and flowing water. If you're living with a tight-quarters bathroom with few amenities, take notes from this bathroom redesign and expand into an adjacent space.

ROOM FOR EXPANSION

Adding on is a costly proposition—but fortunately it's not the only solution for gaining square footage. Look instead at

Although the rest of this 1950s ranch is bright and airy, the bathroom *below* was dark, cramped, and outdated.

BEFORE

An atrium window with a view to a meditation garden makes soaking in the bathtub *above* a visual and tactile treat. A flip of a switch causes water to flow from the fountain.

A feature as uncomplicated as this tubside niche *left* can make a bathroom more comfortable. (For more ways to bring comfort into your bath, turn to page 126.)

rooms surrounding the bathroom to see if you can borrow space for expansion.

Although the homeowner said from the beginning that a linen closet in the hall could merge into this bathroom to make it bigger, designer Linda expanded on the idea. By pushing the sink wall 2 feet into the adjacent bedroom (plus incorporating the old linen closet) the bathroom gains spaciousness. (For ideas on expanding your bathroom's boundaries, see "Exploring Space" *opposite top right*.)

WET ZONE

Once you've captured the square footage you need, determine how you want to put it to the best use. Is storage high on your wish list? Maybe you want a "super vanity" with dual sinks, ample counter space, and a cosmetics station. Or, if you're like this homeowner, bathing and showering earn top priorities. If that's the case dedicate the space to a smartly designed "wet zone," such as the abutting tub and shower *left*.

Replacing the shallow tub is an extra-deep tub selected especially for long, hot soaks. A wide ledge, tiled niche, and bamboo shelf surround the tub and stow spa amenities. The shower relocates from the entry area of the bathroom to the exterior wall perpendicular to the tub

Modern convenience meets serenity in this bathroom redo, accomplished by bumping the vanity side of the room 2 feet into an adjacent bedroom (see the floor plan *opposite*). Maple cabinetry, slate counters and flooring, and glass tiles combine to make this a tranquil retreat *top left* and *above*.

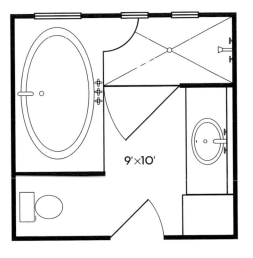

THE **PLAN**

Bumping the vanity wall out *below* to borrow 2 feet from the adjoining bedroom and incorporating the linen closet gave this master bath the square footage needed for the desired amenities.

9'×10'

EXPLORING SPACE

WHEN YOU DISCOVER that your bath territory is too tight, scout out adjacent areas:

CLOSETS. Capture closet space from a bedroom or hallway and make up for the lost storage with smarter organizational solutions inside the bath. (For storage ideas turn to page 24.)

HALLWAYS. Incorporate hallway space into the bathroom and relocate the bath entry, if necessary. This solution works especially well if your bath is at the end of a hallway.

BEDROOMS. Look at the Before and After photos of this bathroom to see proof that just a few feet borrowed from a bedroom can make a huge difference in efficiency and comfort.

BUMP OUT. If you can't find adjacent space to borrow, an addition doesn't have to be huge to make a difference. For example add an 18- to 24-inch-deep bump-out to accommodate a larger tub and/or shower.

Glass 4×4-inch tiles line the shower and the walls of the "wet zone" *below,* which includes the bathtub surround. Designer Linda Maglia wisely asked the homeowner to first view the tiles on a sample board with grout in place, pointing out that the choice of grout can greatly alter the look of the tile.

opposite bottom. One end of the shower features a bench abutting the tub, which allows a bather to sit, swing around, and step into the shower and vice versa.

Opposite the bathtub, a long vanity features an oversize sink that mimics the curvaceous shape of the tub. A wall-mounted faucet and cross handles are reminiscent of the tub filler for additional visual continuity.

ANOTHER DIMENSION
Light fulfills an important role in enhancing the spaciousness of the bath. Recessed downlights, for example, illuminate each primary area: tub, shower, vanity, entry area, and separate toilet

compartment. At the end of the bathroom, a new atrium window pairs with two smaller windows to introduce light and views to the tub and shower areas. A mirror stretches across the length of the vanity, multiplying the power of the natural and artificial sources of light and making the room feel even larger.

Glass tiles, in a subtle shade reminiscent of chamomile tea, bring yet another dimension to the shower and bathtub surround. The eye picks up on the transparency of the material, creating the illusion of additional depth.

For more ideas on selecting a bathtub, turn the page.

SOOTHING SOAKS

Love the tub featured on pages 54–57? Let these ideas inspire you to create your own blissful bathing experience.

DELUXE DUET Create a custom-built tub on site, such as this one *below*, which features a marble surround and shaped seats for two people. The bathtub anchors one entire end of the bathroom and takes in a view of the lake.

PRIVACY FIRST If you don't have a privacy fence right outside your tub window, such as the bathroom on pages 54–57, consider this alternative. Frosted glass allays privacy concerns in this high-profile setting *above* and repeats on the walls of the flanking shower stall (on the left) and toilet room (on the right).

TV TIME The owner of this bathroom *above* wanted a deep soaking tub and a television so she could relax and watch baseball games. Low-voltage technology makes the television safe for a bath.

TUB TALK

AS A PRIMARY COMPONENT in your bath, the tub deserves these special considerations to ensure great function and style.

ALL AROUND. Address the areas surrounding your tub. To create a focal point or capture a view, tubs often combine with windows for a dramatic presentation. Make sure window treatments or garden structures let you take in the view without others seeing you. Your tub surround can add both luxury and convenience by providing a place to set towels and to sit.

WARM THOUGHTS. To make sure you have enough hot water for your bath, your home water heater should have at least two-thirds the capacity of your tub. With a jetted tub, an in-line or passive heater helps maintain water temperature.

BUY BIG ENOUGH. Bathtubs may be the most underused fixtures installed in master baths, often because homeowners have a model that's the wrong size. Shape is not a big concern, but the length is if you want to lounge. The standard width for whirlpool tubs is 36 inches; go with at least a 42-inch-wide model a minimum of 6 feet long if you have the space. (See the bathtub templates on pages 185–186 for help in determining if the bathtub you want will fit your space.)

WHIRLPOOLS VERSUS AIR TUBS. If you want moving water in your bath, your main choice is between a whirlpool tub and an air tub. Although the two pamper similarly, it helps to understand the basic differences. In a whirlpool tub it's the circulation of water, usually by built-in jets and hoses, that provides the massage. No water circulates through an air bath system. Air baths were first used in hospitals for their therapeutic effect.

With a whirlpool a bather can usually adjust the air and water flow of the individual jets or control their overall force at the pump. The number of jets in a tub can vary and isn't always the most important factor; power is important too. A few powerful jets may move the same amount of water as several less-powerful ones. In an air bath hole placement—which is fixed—determines the massage action.

Keep in mind that less adjustable air baths may be easier to clean. An automatic purge feature forces additional air out of the holes after the water drains. This clears the holes and also dries the air chamber and tub. If oils and gels are part of your bath ritual, check with a dealer about restrictions on their use. Because no water circulates through it, an air bath can withstand bath products without clogging; most whirlpools cannot.

Finally consider noise. Both whirlpools and air tubs can be loud. Expect 70 to 80 decibels, depending on how fast the motor and pumps work. That's about the same level as regular street traffic or a quiet train.

SIT AND SOAK. If you find still waters more soothing, a soaking tub may be your preference, but make sure it is comfortable. Purchase a soaking tub deep enough—about 20 to 22 inches—so you don't have to scrunch down.

You couldn't help but feel a little regal relaxing in this bathtub, which is crowned with a barrel-vault ceiling and stylishly guarded by four impressive columns. The large window lets in an abundance of sunlight; the glass-block design ensures privacy.

ROYAL TREATMENT

If your home is your castle, why not treat yourself like royalty with a master bathroom equipped for comfort?

As with the bathtub, the waterfall in this shower *right* features a sequence of colored lights designed to relax or stimulate. (See "Built-In Color Therapy" *below*.) The violet light shown is said to be inspirational and creative.

This shower enclosure *far right*, equipped with water jets, a waterfall, and colored lights, also features a standard showerhead for a traditional soap-and-water shower. The enclosure fits neatly into a corner and closes tightly to retain heat and spray.

FORTUNATELY YOUR MASTER bathroom doesn't have to be castle-size to fit in amenities that allow you to pamper yourself splendidly. The builder of this new house visits home builder shows around the country to find fabulous new features to help him transform the bathroom into a spalike retreat. You can gather similar ideas and see the latest in fixtures, fittings, cabinetry, and surfaces by touring local kitchen and bath showrooms and new home showhouses. Take notes from this bath to acquire the ultimate showering and bathing experience.

HEAVENLY SOAKS

When you visit a bath showroom, you'll find jetted and non-jetted (soaking) tubs in a tremendous variety of shapes, sizes, and color. (For more information on bathtubs,

BUILT-IN COLOR THERAPY

BUILDER JIM HARMEYER of Tyler Homes doesn't necessarily believe that more is better, especially when it comes to square footage in the bathroom. "People today have the kind of lifestyles that they're calling for more details, conveniences, and amenities and less square footage," he says. So Jim seeks out special features that offer greater impact without gobbling up floor space.

In this bathroom a corner shower makes up for the space requirements of the oversize bathtub. Both the tub and shower offer a variety of pampering features, including some interesting "light therapy." These models each feature fiber-optic lights that cast different colors and are said to relax or invigorate, depending on the color emitted.

Some research shows that color and light affect your mood. For example, it is believed that warm colors stimulate your mood whereas cool colors make you feel calm. The bathtub and shower in this bathroom automatically produce a sequence of colors; if you like a particular color, you can push a button so it stays on while you bathe or shower.

THE PLAN

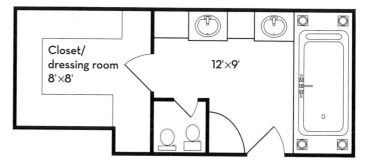

Closet/
dressing room
8'×8'

12'×9'

This bath *above* offers high
style and luxurious amenities
in a relatively small space.

As water spills from the waterfall *above*, you
can lean against the built-in pillow and allow
the warm stream to flow around your neck
and shoulders. Fiber optic colored lighting
also emits from the waterfall area.

turn to pages 58–59.) Ask questions
about the features available on the various
models. And don't be shy about taking
off your shoes and climbing into a tub.
Although you can't experience the water
jets and other features without getting
wet, you can at least test it for fit and
comfort. Take home this extra-large
bathtub *left*, for example, and lean your
head against the built-in pillow; turn
on the waterfall that flows from beneath
the pillow to massage your neck. Water
flow from jets within the tub can be
adjusted from vigorous bursts of water
for a soothing massage to gentle streams
designed to make you feel calm and
relaxed. To heighten your soaking

experience, build a wide ledge around the tub for holding candles, scented oils, and fluffy towels. This bathtub offers the added benefits of an attractive tile border, a barrel-vault ceiling, and four towering columns, which extend from the tub deck to the ceiling.

WAKE-UP SHOWER

If you don't have time for a long soak in the morning, equip your master bathroom with a shower that's outfitted with body sprays and specially designed showerheads. (For more showering options, turn to page 18.) In the fully enclosed shower in this bathroom, the experience includes your choice of powerful massaging jets, a relaxing waterfall, or a combination of both. You can also gradually increase the power of the water jets as you shower.

STORAGE AND MORE

There's more to a royal pampering affair than tubs and showers, of course. Design your bathroom with sinks and vanities for two and enough storage for towels and other items. This master bathroom offers a lower countertop between dual vanities. The cushioned seat becomes a comfortable place to apply cosmetics and do your hair. A floor-to-ceiling cabinet at one end of the vanities offers enough storage to make a linen closet unnecessary. Directly across from this cabinet, a private compartment houses a toilet and a bidet. Turn the page for more information on toilets and bidets.

Granite countertops and honey-stained maple cabinetry make the vanity area *above* as elegant as the rest of the bathroom. A storage tower on the left and storage within the vanities ensure there's a place for everything. A stool pulls up to the lower countertop for performing morning and evening rituals.

TOILETS AND BIDETS

When it's time to think about the toilet or bidet for your bath (the bath on pages 60–63 boasts a bidet), consider these ideas and options.

PRIVACY, PLEASE There's more than one way to provide privacy for the toilet. In this space *above* elegant floor-to-ceiling bronze-color silk curtain panels draw closed to conceal the toilet compartment.

BEHIND CLOSED DOORS In a shared space, such as this master bathroom *below*, the toilet occupies a separate room with a door for the ultimate in privacy.

TOILET TALK

TOILETS COME IN AN AMAZING ARRAY of styles, colors, materials, and sizes. Good-quality toilets start at about $300 and run up into the thousands. Believe it or not, there's even a $5,000 toilet designed in solid ash to look like a throne. When you raise the lid, the throne plays music; a candleholder and ashtray are built into the armrests. Visit a bath showroom or browse online to see some of these other special toilet features:

ROYAL FLUSH. Some new models promise virtually clog-free operation.

HIP CHOICES. Manufacturers continue to develop sleeker styles and industrial looks that even include models fashioned from stainless steel.

KID FRIENDLY. For a household with children, consider installing toilets sized for them.

BLISSFUL BOTTOMS. For the ultimate in comfort and cleanliness, check out heated seats and seats equipped with personal hygiene systems (see "Bidets" *below*).

LIDS TO LOVE. There will be no more concerns about finding the lid up when you select a seat that automatically lowers after the flush.

EASY CLEAN. Wall-mounted toilets make it easier to clean the floor beneath the unit.

ONE-PIECE TOILETS. Unbroken lines make one-piece toilets easier to clean than two-piece models. Their wider bowls require less scrubbing than narrow ones associated with two-piece toilets because the wider design does a better job of clearing waste. Toilets with straight sides that hide the bolts securing the unit to the floor are also easier to wipe clean than models with lots of lumps and bumps.

BIDETS. A bidet is a small, low sink used for partial bathing. Sit astride the bowl facing the faucet to fill the bowl or control the spray. There are basically two types of bidets: those that fill from above the rim and those that fill from below. An above-the-rim model will have hot and cold faucets, either wall-mounted or at the side and a stopper. You run the water and fill the bidet, then sit.

Below-the-rim bidets usually have the controls on the rim and an opening at the bottom with a "rosette" spray device to spray water up, fountainlike. The sprays are cleansing.

Because below-the-rim bidets have inlets under the water, a clogged overflow or sudden drop in water pressure could cause contaminated water to be sucked back into freshwater lines. To prevent contamination a bidet must be outfitted with vacuum-breaker or antisiphon devices. All recently manufactured bidets are so equipped, but vintage products usually are not.

Often designed to coordinate with the toilet, bidets run $325 to $1,300, depending on color, style, and operating techniques. The spray types are usually at the upper end.

Replacement seats that function like a bidet are available for standard toilets. They include warm-water sprays and heating for the seat. These personal hygiene systems start at about $350.

BRIGHT FUTURE

With a little extra planning and forethought, your bathroom can accommodate your needs both now and in the future.

Once a spare bedroom, a pair of empty nesters converted this space *opposite* into the bath of their dreams. Located on the main floor just a few steps from the master bedroom, the bath is beautiful and accommodating to people of all ages and abilities. Separate his and her vanities are located on adjacent walls. His vanity, shown here, stands beside the spacious walk-in shower.

Walkways measuring 42 inches wide and door openings that are 36 inches wide make this bathroom comfortable for two people and easily accessible for a wheelchair, if necessary.

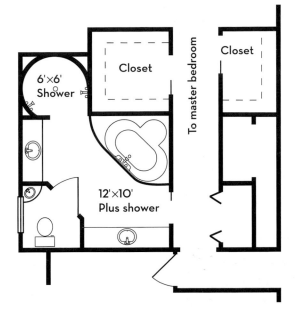

6'×6' Shower

Closet

Closet

To master bedroom

12'×10' Plus shower

THE BEST BATHS are comfortable and inviting whether you use the space as a personal retreat or frequently share it with a messy toddler, a primping teenager, or a busy spouse. To ensure your bath meets both today's and tomorrow's needs, incorporate these accommodating strategies in your bath plan. (For even more information on accessible baths, see pages 72–77.)

EASY PASSAGE

Generous aisles enable family members to pass through the space without bumping elbows. They also provide room for a baby carrier to safely sit should you need to keep an eye on a little one while you're grooming. A walkway width of 42 inches or more also ensures accessibility for wheelchairs should any family member ever need to use one. As shown in the plan *top right* all walkways in this bath are 42 inches wide and door openings are 36 inches wide, including the bath entrance

door, toilet compartment door, and shower threshold. The extra aisle width does not require a sacrifice to style. The fine furniture cabinetry details and stone-look ceramic tile surfaces make the open bath as attractive as it is hardworking.

GROOMING ROOM

Most designers recommend a counter length of at least 3 feet for a single user and at least 5 feet for shared counter space. If you have room install separate vanities as shown in this bath so you can claim personal space. The vanities in this bath are ultra accommodating. "His" vanity *opposite* is 5 feet long and includes a pair of appliance garages that keeps the counters clutter-free. "Her" vanity, shown on page 69, is 6½ feet long and provides storage for all her grooming items as well as cleaning products. Tiled mirror frames create a decorative focal point for each vanity. (To learn how to frame a bath mirror with tile, see page 158.)

Form and function unite in this clever tub design *above*. The rounded whirlpool is ergonomically designed and features a seat in the tub deck for resting outside the water while soaking only your feet.

LOTS OF LIGHT

TO LIGHT A roomy bath like this one, you'll need to include a combination of light fixtures. Here several downlights combine with two wall-mounted fixtures installed above the tile-framed mirror at each vanity. The bath also includes excellent night lighting with a fixture installed inside each vanity base cabinet. The light shines through the translucent glass sinks, providing beautiful nighttime illumination. (For more advice on bath lighting, see pages 30–31.)

Texture and two paint tones give the walls *above* a comfortably aged look. (To learn how to add this finish to your walls, see page 156.)

COMFORT AMENITIES

To bring even more comfort into your bath, add an amenity that you or others who share the space have always wanted. In this bath that translates into a large whirlpool tub featuring a safety grab bar and a seat outside the tub, enabling the users to soak just their feet. The shower is equally as roomy and comfortable; the round stall measures 6 feet in diameter, which is large enough for a wheelchair to turn around should it ever become necessary. The doorless opening eliminates the need for glass cleaning.

EASY CLEAN

In addition to installing a doorless shower you can reduce the time you spend on cleanup (a bonus for growing families or retirees) by choosing surfaces like the ones in this bath, which disguise water spots and fingerprints and rinse clean in minutes. Here slip-resistant, matte-finish tiles cover the floor, tub, and shower surround and don't require frequent cleaning. (Slip-resistant tiles also provide better traction for a wheelchair.) Diamond-shaped decorative tiles add cheerful color without compromising function. Wipe-clean solid surfacing tops the vanities. As with the tiles, the matte surface disguises spots. The eloquent glass sinks require a little more maintenance but the high style they add is worth the extra wipe down.

For more information on sinks and faucets, turn the page.

The toilet compartment *top* is a half-bath by itself—a small sink across from the toilet makes hygiene convenient.

The open shower *above* is roomy enough for two and features both a handheld and an adjustable wall-mounted showerhead.

Translucent glass sinks bring high style to the vanity counters and beautifully complement the accent tiles used around the mirror and on the tub and shower.

SAVVY SINKS AND FAUCETS

Love the sinks shown in the bath on pages 66–69? Look here to find the right sink and faucet for your bath.

VESSEL Available in models to fit any bath, above-counter bowl-style sinks carry a few design considerations. These seemingly freestanding bowls come in glass, porcelain, metal, and wood and sit higher than a standard sink, so you need to adjust the countertop height accordingly. The faucet typically mounts on the wall and must be placed at the right height to minimize splashing. This half-vessel model *above* requires a single-hole, sink-mounted faucet.

ANTIQUE OR REPRODUCTION MODELS

Ideal for vintage or traditional styled baths, freestanding sink tables, as shown *below* and in the bath on pages 144–147, come with legs and a built-in countertop. Some models have a built-in sink; others are designed for a vessel, undermount, or drop-in sink addition. Plumbing is visible.

UNDERMOUNT Installed in a countertop hole just smaller than its rim, this undermount sink *above*, from the bath featured on pages 46–51, seems to float beneath the counter for an uncluttered look and easy surface cleaning.

SELF-RIMMING The easiest type of sink to install, the self-rimming sink *above* and on pages 66–69 features a rim that rests on the countertop; the basin drops below the counter.

FAUCET FUNCTION

FIND A FAUCET that matches the style of your bath and the space you have allotted.

SPREAD-FIT FAUCETS. These faucets *near left top* have a separate spout and handles. They can be adapted to fit holes spaced several inches apart. For example, the spout can be placed on a rear corner, and the handles off to one side as shown. These faucets are handy for tight installations where there is not enough room for a full faucet at the back of the sink.

CONTEMPORARY SINGLE LEVER. These faucets *near left center* have one spout and one handle that controls the flow of both hot and cold water. They are ideal for people with limited mobility.

WALL-MOUNTED FAUCETS. This faucet type as shown *near left bottom*, attaches to the wall as opposed to the sink or the counter. These faucets were designed for unusually shaped sinks, such as vessels or old-fashion farm sinks modified for use in the bath.

ACCESSIBLE BEAUTY

You can have a bathroom that's as snazzy as it is easy to navigate—no matter your abilities.

Colorful, lively tile patterns and a chartreuse chest of drawers prevent this barrier-free bath from feeling "institutional." The homeowners chose this cabinet because its drawers roll open easily. You could equip cabinetry with roll-out wire bins or shelves for easier access. Hexagonal tiles on the floor suit the era of the home and are also slip resistant.

Solid-surfacing brackets support the matching countertop that encircles the shallow sink *right*. Using brackets instead of obtrusive legs allows a wheelchair user to pull up closer to the sink.

SIMPLIFY YOUR DAILY ROUTINE and complement your sense of style by designing a bathroom that stylishly eliminates barriers—a smart strategy whether you break your leg skiing, use a wheelchair, or plan to live in your house throughout your lifetime.

SPACE PLANNING

If you're building a new home, design a bath spacious enough to allow easy mobility for a wheelchair user. Or, if you are planning an accessible bath for an existing home, borrow square footage from surrounding spaces. That was the case for this 1938 house when the homeowners merged the existing bathroom with two closets and the sitting area of an adjoining bedroom. The result is a 21×7-foot bathroom designed to complement the style of the house while accommodating a wheelchair user.

BATHING WITH EASE

Incorporate an open shower in your design, creating a wide entry with no door or no raised threshold so a wheelchair user or someone with limited mobility can easily enter the shower. For this bathroom the former closets became the new 5×5-foot shower with a stylish white and blue tile curved wall. A wheelchair user can roll into the shower and transfer to a movable bench inside (see page 77). One adjustable showerhead and one stationary head allow

The rim of the sink *above* juts beyond the countertop, providing easier access to someone who is seated. The drain is at the back corner of the sink, allowing the pipes below to be installed out of the way of someone in a wheelchair.

BARRIER-FREE BATHS

THE GOAL of a barrier-free bath is to make all users as independent and as comfortable as possible. Even if no one in your home has special needs now, planning a bath that can accommodate wheelchairs and walkers can make guests—or even a kid with a cast—feel more welcome and comfortable.

LOCATION. Creating a barrier-free bath starts first with the location. It should be situated on the ground floor of the house to avoid stairs.

DOOR SIZE. Plan for a clear door opening of 34–38 inches. Larger openings are hard to open and close from a seated position, and narrower openings make it difficult, if not impossible, for a wheelchair to get through.

HANDLE SELECTION. Equip entrance doors, drawers, and faucets with lever or D-shape handles. They are easier to operate than knobs, especially for young children and people with arthritis or limited mobility.

FLOOR SPACE. For a typical-size wheelchair to make a complete turnaround, leave a circular area of clear floor space measuring 5 feet in diameter. Leave an area in front of the sink that measures at least 30×48 inches (although the clear floor space can overlap). Toilets need a clear floor space that is 48 inches square. Bathtubs need a clear floor space of 60×60 inches in front of the tub.

SHOWER STALLS. Shower stalls should measure at least 4 feet square with an opening at least 36 inches wide. Include a bench or seat that is 17–19 inches above the floor to make it easier for someone to transfer from a wheelchair to the bench.

FOR MORE INFORMATION see "More Barrier-Free Guidelines" on page 77.

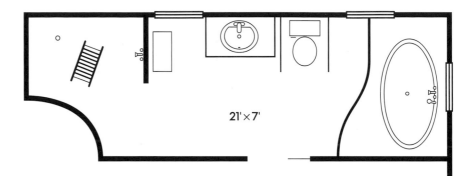

THE **PLAN**

This barrier-free bath *below* features wide aisles and numerous amenities, ensuring comfort for all who use it.

21'×7'

water sprays at practically any height. (A handheld showerhead can also be added to an existing shower.)

When including a bathtub in your accessible bathroom plans, provide a wide deck around the tub for sitting and to serve as a place for keeping toiletries and towels close by. The tub in this bathroom, for example, features a wide, sweeping ledge that allows a person to sit on the edge and pivot to enter it.

PERSONAL HYGIENE

To ensure a barrier-free vanity, keep floor space open in front of the sink and allow knee space below. This bathroom positions the vanity and toilet side-by-side on the wall between the shower and tub. Both the solid-surfacing countertop and the shallow vitreous-china sink hang low on the wall, rather than supported by obtrusive legs. Plumbing pipes angle back toward the wall to allow for more unobstructed knee room. The mirror above the sink tilts down so someone seated can use it as well.

Allocate plenty of space to maneuver around the toilet and install grab bars on each side of the seat. The toilet in this bathroom also offers a bidet feature for hands-free hygienic needs.

For more ideas on making a bathroom accessible and barrier-free, turn the page.

Ample space in front of the toilet and beside the bathtub provides room for maneuvering a wheelchair. Tiles feature color throughout the thickness of the material so if anything drops on the floor or the tiles on the surround get bumped, the damage won't be as noticeable.

MORE BARRIER–FREE IDEAS

Ingenious products and well-thought-out plans make today's accessible baths, such as the one shown on pages 72–75, visually appealing and easy for everyone to use.

as the one shown on pages 72–75,

FUNCTION FIRST

SAFE TILES Small hexagonal floor tiles are attractive and slip resistant. Selecting tiles with color throughout the material ensures that any damage won't show as easily.

ANGLED SOLUTION A pulley system and crank allow this mirror *above* to hang flat against the wall or tilt downward to accommodate someone who is seated.

LOOP OPTIONS The support bars beside the toilet *below* are looped to offer an upper and a lower handle. Someone shorter can use the lower handle, whereas someone taller can grasp the upper one. The bars can be turned to hang flat against the wall when not in use. A bidet system attached to the toilet allows for hands-free hygiene.

SHOWER SAVVY The freestanding shower bench *above* offers more flexibility than a built-in version. It's designed not to tip over. Reinforcements in the walls enable the grab bars to bear significant weight. Large faucet handles simplify grasping. A vertical bar allows the adjustable showerhead to slide up and down to accommodate either a standing or seated person.

TUBSIDE SEATS One end of the tub ledge narrows to fit beside the toilet; the wider portion can be used for sitting, storage, or display *left*.

MORE BARRIER-FREE GUIDELINES

YOU CAN DESIGN a bathroom to meet changing accessibility needs. Here's how:

FUTURE NEEDS. During the remodeling or building phase, specify extra structural supports in the ceiling above the tub. This allows future installation of an electric lift should you need one. Likewise you can specify extra supports in walls inside the shower and beside the toilet so grab bars can be installed later, if needed. If you install 3/4-inch plywood sheathing over the studs from floor to ceiling, you can then install grab bars anywhere on the walls as needed. This way you won't have to spend extra money to tear out a wall and add framing.

GRAB BARS. If you install grab bars now, they can offer stability for all users, and when not in use they can double as towel bars. Lever-style door handles and faucet controls are easier to operate by anyone with limited mobility. Install shower controls so you can reach them inside and outside the stall. Put the controls 38–48 inches above the floor and above the grab bar if there is one.

HEAD'S UP. Install a handheld showerhead no higher than 48 inches above the floor at its lowest position so it is reachable when sitting.

SAFETY. Anti-scald faucets reduce scalding risks for children and adults. Or turn the hot water heater down to 120 degrees. To prevent cuts and bruises, add a cushion to the tub spout. Round the countertop, bath surround, and cabinetry corners. Choose slip-resistant flooring and rugs with a nonslip backing. To prevent electrocution all electrical outlets should be on ground fault-circuit interrupters.

STORAGE STRATEGY. For maximum open floor space, eliminate closets or built-in storage from your plan. This way you can purchase movable pieces of furniture and change the layout if your storage needs increase.

WINDOWS. Casement windows are the easiest to operate from a wheelchair. Install windows 24 to 30 inches above the floor so wheelchair users can open, close, and easily see out of them.

Occupants of this freestanding tub can take in hillside views through a wall of windows as they relax. A handheld spray makes rinsing easy.

RETREAT FOR TWO

Pamper yourself and your mate morning and night in a spacious bath filled with resortlike amenities.

A towel-warming drawer *right*, operating much like a warming drawer found in a kitchen, heats up the spalike spirit of this indulgent space. Just steps from the limestone-tile shower and the central vanity island, the drawer supplies toasty after-shower and post-shaving wraps.

IF THE BATH SPACE you have is too small to comfortably accommodate two, convert a spare bedroom into a private bath oasis. This 15×16-foot bedroom-sized bath features everything from a coffee bar to a makeup center. To make good use of a large, almost-square space, the designer laid out the room more like she would a hardworking kitchen than a basic bath. To make your bath equally as accommodating, put some of the function-focused ideas shown on the following pages to work for you.

BACK-TO-BACK VANITIES

Instead of leaving a lot of empty floor space in the middle of a large bath, incorporate a center island. As in a kitchen, an island breaks up the space and reduces steps between functional centers while keeping the layout of the room interesting. The bath island shown on page 81 includes a pair of back-to-back vanities, each equipped with a sink, ample counter space, and two banks of drawers.

AMENITY CENTERS

Placing the vanities in the middle of the room frees up wall space for function-packed centers, much like the work centers in a well-designed kitchen. Match these centers to your personal wishes, such as a sauna for relaxing or a weight machine for working out. Here amenity centers include a makeup vanity and a built-in storage armoire complete with a warming drawer for heating towels. There is also a shower for two and a freestanding soaking tub with remote-controlled whirlpool jets.

ETHEREAL ATMOSPHERE

Once you have a layout in hand, focus your attention on the atmosphere of the room. (For more bath plans, see pages 36–37.)

A coffee bar *above*, complete with a sink and undercounter refrigerator, sits near the entrance to the master bedroom. The location enables the couple to grab a cup of coffee or a snack without making a trip to the kitchen. Don't have the room or the budget for a mini-kitchen? Top a rolling cart with a coffeemaker and your favorite bean blends.

Across from "her" side of the center island, a smaller vanity provides a place to store and apply cosmetics.

For a peaceful feel, choose a neutral palette warmed with a variety of textures. Here honed-limestone tile floors dotted with bronze tiles provide textural contrast against the polished granite counters and creamy glazed cabinets. Glass doors on the cabinets promote a light and airy openness while showcasing colorful accessories chosen for their relaxing qualities—from candles and bath salts to coffee cups and bath towels. The result is a bath that is beautiful in both form and function— proof positive that you can have it all.

For more information on filling your bath with spalike elements, turn the page.

THE **PLAN**

Make a bedroom-turned-bath into a retreat for two with centered vanities and a variety of amenity centers. This bath plan *below* includes a sit-down vanity, a coffee bar, a private toilet compartment, and a built-in storage armoire.

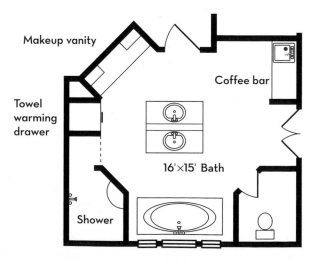

Makeup vanity

Coffee bar

Towel warming drawer

16'×15' Bath

Shower

In this detail-oriented bath, faucets and light fixtures feature an oil-rubbed bronze finish, linking them to the bronze inset tiles on the floor and shower walls. At the island the countertops on both sides of the center mirrors provide space for toiletries.

AT-HOME RESORT

Come home to a resort experience every day when you shape a bathroom around amenities like these—and those shown on pages 78–81.

MIRROR, MIRROR A pretty magnifying mirror *below* is an inexpensive amenity that makes applying makeup easier on the eyes and enables you to take a peek at the back of your hairdo. For full-body checkups install a floor-to-ceiling mirror on the back of a door or on an open wall in or near the bath.

ELEGANT ACCENTS Make a space look special with accents. Splurge on a few glamorous touches such as mirrored tiles and shiny fixtures, such as the wall sconce *above*, that turn a bath into pure luxury.

THERE'S MORE TO A SPA-STYLE bathroom than an oversize whirlpool tub. For a complete retreat add these amenities:

MUSIC MASTERS. Build in a stereo system with miniature speakers that set on shelves or tuck into a cabinet.

HAPPY FEET. Warm your feet with an in-floor heating system and soften your landing with plush, toe-tickling rugs.

PERSONALITY PLUS. Accessorize with artwork and collectibles you love.

SOAPS AND OILS. Infuse your bath with your favorite scents to make you feel invigorated at the start of the day or relaxed before bedtime.

BEAUTIFUL BLOOMS Fresh flowers aren't limited to the living room. Bring a bouquet *below* into the bath to brighten dreary days.

THICK AND THIRSTY White towels *above*, like the ones you might find in a luxury hotel, make you feel like you're always on a vacation. Keep plenty on hand and include a towel-warming bar discussed on page 15 (or a warming drawer shown on page 79) to provide toasty towels after bathing or showering.

A **BATH** FOR EVERY **STYLE**

Your bathroom can be as eye-appealing and personal as any room in the house. Use this collection of baths to discover or confirm the look you want to bring into your new space, whether it is richly detailed and elegant, streamlined and soothing, or splashed with fun for kids or the entire family. Peruse these pages to see baths soaked in bold color, calming neutrals, and every combination in between. This section will teach you how to incorporate the elements of a favorite scheme into your own bath using surfaces, paint, fabric, accessories, furnishings, and more.

TRADITIONAL POLISH

To create a timeless traditional look, fill your bath with finely crafted cabinets and sleek, natural surfaces.

ARTFULLY CRAFTED, traditional-style baths like the one featured here never go out of style. Symmetrical arrangements of cabinetry and fixtures create a feeling of balance and order. Architectural details include deep crown moldings, customary chair rails, finely crafted woodwork, and lustrous natural surfaces. Here handcrafted cabinets made from reclaimed heart pine combine with stretches of limestone and a spacious layout, encouraging occupants to relax and enjoy the craftsmanship.

LINES AND CURVES

A pleasing combination of gentle curves and rectilinear shapes is also part of the look, as illustrated by the oval-shaped tub deck and mirrors and the square cabinetry panels *opposite*. Color is often in a mid-range of tones, although very dark and

Encased in centuries-old heart pine, this island tub *opposite* provides two of the best seats in the house. French limestone tiles in two color waves fashion patterned wainscoting, backsplashes, and soffits on top of the honey-hue walls, creating a visual link to the limestone counters, tub deck, and floor.

Vanities stand opposite one another, creating design symmetry and allowing plenty of room to get ready for the day. Heightened countertops on both vanities provide comfort. Burnished heart-pine cabinets, brass fixtures, honey-tone walls, and liberal use of light-reflecting mirrors combine for a classic traditional ambience.

very light hues can also be used; neons and brights don't mix. Typically the fabrics come from high-quality natural materials, including fine silks, heavy linens, and rich wools. Vintage-looking rugs in this bath create softness underfoot and provide textural contrast against the smooth stone floors. (Avoid using natural wool or vintage rugs in wet areas—choose washable cottons and nylons instead.) As the rugs illustrate, time-proven botanicals are a popular choice, though tone-on-tone and small all-over patterns are also common. For window treatments look for wooden shutters or pleated draperies with top valances and undersheers. Because this bath is located on a secluded property, the windows remain bare, allowing the handcrafted casings to be seen.

FINISHING TOUCHES

The vertical light rails framing the mirrors in this bath are an unexpected element that make the area more personal. Although not part of the plan for this bath, wall sconces are commonplace and often supplemented with simple recessed fixtures or a centered chandelier. Accessories here, as in most traditional settings, include urns, plants, framed artwork, and vases. Heirlooms and antiques further personalize the look and bring more coziness to the space. For additional personal touches that will make your bath feel like an at-home retreat, turn the page.

TRADITIONAL ELEMENTS

NATURALLY LUSTROUS SURFACES, such as marble, granite, or limestone counters, and wood plank or stone tile floors.

CABINETRY WITH RAISED PANELS sporting natural wood, richly stained wood, or a painted and glazed finish.

CLASSIC FABRIC PATTERNS, such as florals, botanicals, checks, plaids, tone-on-tone stripes, and solids.

VINTAGE ACCESSORIES, including shiny metal hardware, sconces, urns, framed prints, hand-painted ceramics, and cut-glass bottles and vases.

To see a more formal classically styled bath, turn to page 116.

For more information on **traditional style**, visit *HGTV.com/designstyles*

The snack bar *left* furthers the feeling of making the master bath an at-home haven. The bar is outfitted with a mini-refrigerator, sink, and microwave oven. Traditional accessories include a classic framed print, antique Majolica, and a brass sink and faucet.

PERSONAL INDULGENCE

As the bath on pages 86–89 illustrates, filling the room with favorite accessories and pampering amenities makes any space feel more intimate and inviting.

MAKEUP SPACE Sit-down vanities provide a spot to pamper yourself daily. In this bath *below* a lowered counter creates a small but convenient makeup table between two sinks. The window located behind the lowered counter draws plenty of natural light—the best light for daytime makeup applications.

BUBBLING BLISS Relax in a luxurious scent-filled bath of bubbles and soak away your cares. Try any of these foaming beauties *above* available at many department stores or online.

CHERISHED ACCESSORIES As the owners of the bath on pages 86–89 did, you can indulge your senses and warm your heart by displaying a few of your favorite things. A 1940s lamp, a pretty bottle of perfume, Victorian brushes, and a favorite baby picture *above* create a very personal display.

91

FRESH FACE

Give a dated bath a casual and friendly attitude with a few easy-to-make surface changes.

Simple additions make this once-barren bath *opposite* feel welcoming. Soft lavender paint warms the walls, a fabric shade softens the window casings, and new brushed-nickel pulls and a fresh coat of paint give the old vanity cabinet an instant update.

PRIOR TO A MAKEOVER, the vanity area *opposite* was less than attractive. A plain mirror, dark-stained oak cabinets, and a worn laminate countertop gave the entire room a dated and uninviting look. If parts of your bath are stuck in the past, create a whole new attitude for the room with a little imagination, a lot of paint, and a few surface updates.

COLOR ADJUSTMENT

To pull your bath into the present, first choose a favorite color as a decorating mainstay, such as the soft lavender used on these bath walls; then select one or two complementary accent colors. This bath uses moss and sage greens as additional accent colors because the hues carry over to other rooms in the house. The pastel color combination creates a warm and soothing atmosphere without overpowering the small room.

Enliven the walls with your favorite color and then extend the hue in varying shades to a few of the more prominent accessories, such as throw rugs and bath towels. Use the accent colors on window treatments, countertops, and additional bath accessories. (For more ways to bring color into a bath, see page 108.)

BRIGHT OUTLOOK

If your work surfaces are not adequately lit, add another light fixture or two. Before the update a single light above the bath mirror filled the grooming area with shadows and glare, making shaving and applying makeup difficult. Now a new three-bulb light bar above the mirror reduces shadows and brightens the whole bath.

Increase natural light with minimal window treatments such as sheer curtain panels or light-filtering Roman shades, as shown *opposite*, which can be pulled open and out of the way. Prior to the remodel block-out panels stopped a great deal of natural light from entering the bath and could never be fully opened due to the short rod length.

SURFACE CHANGES

If your floor or counter tiles are in good shape but the grout is discolored, coat the grout lines with heavy-duty latex paint.

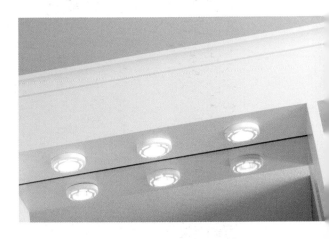

Building a custom frame around the existing mirror *top* provides room for three recessed lights that brighten the mirror and the entire bath.

To bring more color and texture into this casual-style bath, tone-on-tone striped fabric panels are glued to the recessed fronts of the vanity base doors *above*. To make the fabric panels easier to clean, cover them with acrylic plastic. Alternatively you can paint stripes onto the doors.

In lieu of a medicine cabinet, custom-built cubbies *below* frame the vertical sides of the mirror and hold three halogen tract lights in place across the mirror top (shown on page 93). Rolled towels and colorful shower soaps fill the cubbies and bring more color and texture into the room. Less attractive fare is stashed in wicker baskets tucked inside the cubbies.

PAINTING GROUT

GIVE A TILE countertop, floor, or backsplash a whole new look by covering it with heavy-duty latex paint. The paint disguises stains and ground-in dirt and wipes clean with a damp sponge. To paint grout you'll need an artist's brush with a tip narrower than the grout line and heavy-duty latex paint or grout paint (available at paint stores and through Internet outlets). Clean the grout as usual; let dry. Using paint and the artist's brush, evenly apply the paint over the grout lines, taking care to keep the paint within the lines. While the paint is still wet, use a lint-free cloth to wipe any excess paint from the adjoining tiles. Allow the paint to dry thoroughly before using the material as usual. Note that some paint might absorb into the porous grout as the paint cures, so a few touchups may be necessary.

SPLASHY BACKSPLASH

OFTEN OVERLOOKED in the bath, backsplashes offer an easy way to bring more color and style to the walls. In this bath two rows of white tiles dotted with a few decorative lavender diamonds give the backsplash a stylish attitude. If you opt for a painted backsplash finish, coat the area with polyacrylic sealer, which enables you to clean the area with ease. Another option: Attach acrylic plastic to the wall behind the sink to protect the wall finish and make cleanup a breeze.

Here lavender lines match the decorative backsplash tiles. (For advice on painting grout lines, see "Painting Grout," *opposite.*)

Update a worn vanity cabinet with paint, a lively tiled backsplash, and a new countertop. A coat of primer and two coats of pale sage green paint make this vanity base look fresh and new. A new white and lavender tile backsplash brings color to the vanity area, visually connecting the grooming center to the walls. A moss-green-stained concrete slab replaces old laminate. The matte-finish surface disguises water spots, and a new undermount sink eliminates seams that can attract dirt and hold water, causing mildew. For information on other countertop surfaces, turn the page.

For information on other countertop surfaces, turn the page.

CASUAL ELEMENTS

EASY-CARE SURFACES, including concrete or limestone counters and wood plank or tile floors.

NATURAL WOOD or painted cabinetry with little ornamentation.

CLASSIC FABRIC PATTERNS, such as stripes, checks, plaids, and solids.

UNPRETENTIOUS WINDOW COVERINGS, such as Roman shades or sheer curtain panels.

PASTEL, NEUTRAL, OR BRIGHT COLORS to add a sense of warmth and friendliness.

Elaborate arrangements of flowers and accessories won't do in a casual bath such as this. Instead opt for a simple arrangement with two or three stems of your favorite flowers in a vase that complements the decor of the room as shown *right*.

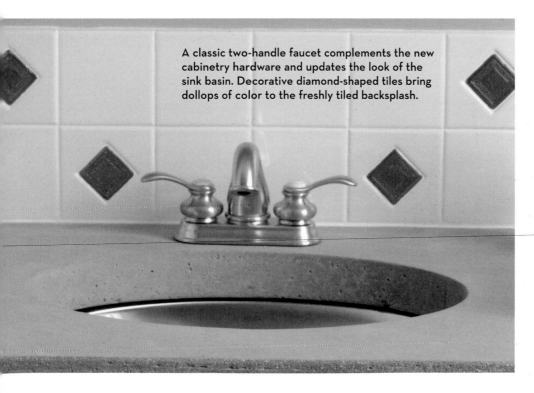

A classic two-handle faucet complements the new cabinetry hardware and updates the look of the sink basin. Decorative diamond-shaped tiles bring dollops of color to the freshly tiled backsplash.

COUNTER TOPPERS

The bath on pages 92–95 received a fresh start with a concrete countertop. Look here to find the surfacing material with the right style and function for your bath.

STONE Prized for natural beauty and durability, stone counters *above* look great and function well in most any style bath. Slabs are more expensive than tiles, but they eliminate grout cleanup. Granite is the least porous of the natural stones, making it one of the better choices for counters. Limestone and marble are more porous and must be sealed often to prevent staining and pitting. Specialty colors and patterns cost more than common varieties.

SOLID SURFACING Made from engineered resin, solid-surfacing countertops *below* (from the bath on pages 32–35) appear seam-free, require little maintenance, and are more durable than laminate. A wide variety of colors, patterns, and stone look-alikes is available. Edge treatments range from a smooth edge that imitates stone to intricate inlaid designs in contrasting colors. Solid surfacing sinks can be integrated directly into the countertop, which means no seams to clean.

CERAMIC TILE Durable and waterproof, ceramic tile *below* and in the bath featured on pages 122–125 comes in a host of colors, patterns, and textures. Some tiles mimic natural stone so perfectly that it is difficult to tell the difference. Prices vary greatly depending on the pattern selected. Tile grout, if left unsealed, can stain. To minimize discoloration, install a tiled countertop using narrow grout joints and a darker color grout.

LAMINATE A budget-priced, low-maintenance surface, plastic laminate *above* offers an array of colors and patterns. Textures range from smooth and glossy to a mottled leatherlike look. Some laminates resemble more expensive natural materials, such as stone or solid surfacing. Resistant to stains, laminate wipes clean with soap and water, but it can wear thin and dull over time.

CONCRETE Concrete *right* can be colored and textured to create many interesting looks. Because the material is very porous, it must be sealed regularly for protection against stains. Hairline cracks are common but do not affect the strength of the material. Slabs can be poured on- or off-site. Prices vary depending on installation requirements and the fabricator you choose. This countertop, featured in the bath on pages 92–95, was made from a do-it-yourself kit purchased online. The kit requires advanced do-it-yourself skills. (For purchasing information, see Credits and Resources beginning on page 188.)

ZEN TREND

Create a soothing and tranquil bath by choosing materials and motifs inspired by Asian design principles.

When the screens are pulled back, the bath and the bedroom feel like one room; the bath opens to bedroom views, artwork, and window ventilation.

JUST AS A PERFECTLY BALANCED Zen garden contains five elements of nature—water, earth, fire, wood, and metal—a Zen bathroom contains representations of each of these elements. (For specific examples of each element as featured in this bath, see *"Feng Shui* Ambience" on page 100.)

Dating back more than 4,000 years, Zen design combines decorating and furnishing principles with ancient Asian philosophy to help people achieve a better balance between work and play, as well as between the private and public areas in a home. As the philosophy suggests, a serene Asian-inspired environment, as this innovative bath displays, offers an antidote to a hectic life. To bring a bit of Zen balance into your bath, follow the lead of this space.

NEUTRAL PALETTE

Neutral colors including white, black, gray, brown, and beige encourage relaxation. To follow the Zen principle of balance as this master suite does, these colors should create a visual balance, using more white than black (because black appears heavier than white) and equal amounts of the medium wood tones, gray, and beige.

When the screens are closed *above,* the bath takes on the feel of a luxurious private getaway. Soft and subdued light filters through the screens and adds a romantic glow when enhanced by candlelight.

An interior addition to a second-floor loft, the soothing Zen bath is now an integral part of a master bedroom suite *right*. Shoji screen partitions—cut from 4×8-foot polycarbonate sheets and mounted on oxidized steel framing—slide open and closed on tracks to make the bath as open or as private as desired.

FENG SHUI AMBIENCE

THIS TRANQUIL BATH was designed by architect Mark Kirkhart to be closely tied to the *Feng Shui* and Zen-friendly design elements of water, earth, fire, wood, and metal. The water zone includes the shower and soaking tub. The earth connection comes from all the natural-looking elements used in the bath, including the faux-slate tub and shower surround as well as the live orchid displayed on the vanity counter. The fire element is met by including a row of votive candles. The wood element comes in by way of the custom-made MDF vanity; the chrome fixtures and faucets provide the final *Feng Shui* component, metal.

TEXTURAL TENACITY

Textures should also be juxtaposed against one another for balance, mixing smooth metal with honed stone or stone look-alikes and earthy woods or wood look-alikes with sleek ceramics. Here smooth-fronted cabinetry crafted from honey-tone lightweight medium-density fiberboard (MDF) combines with a gray honed stone-looking shower and tub surround to create a contemporary Zen environment. (Note that Zen design principles can also be followed within a traditional Asian motif reminiscent of traditional American style.)

Although the shower and tub surround look like cast concrete, they are actually made from lighter-weight faux slate. The faux-slate did not require any additional supports for the existing second-floor joists, as concrete would have, keeping project costs in check. Clean-lined faucets and hardware befit the contemporary Zen style.

PATTERN AND SCALE

As with color and texture, pattern and scale should appear symmetrical and balanced. Rectilinear lines, as illustrated on the Shoji screen walls, are common in a Zen bath. The large pattern complements the commodious scale of the tub and the lengthy vanity.

When accessorizing avoid overdone clusters of knickknacks. A few candles, a live plant, and bathing essentials—as this bath displays—are all the accessories this style necessitates.

NATURAL LIGHT

Filtered light, as opposed to direct sunlight, is another aspect of Zen design, because it encourages tranquility and has a calming effect. The interior location of this bath provides perfect Zen harmony regarding filtered light; the frosted glasslike Shoji screen partitions enable natural light to filter into the space throughout the day.

To discover more about *Feng Shui* and Zen style, turn the page.

Although the vanity area in the bath *above* looks like it is made from maple or another hardwood, it is actually composed of lightweight MDF, a less costly alternative to solid wood. Like the tub and shower, the countertop is faux slate. The mirror runs the full length of the vanity to make the bath feel larger and to reflect more light.

CONTEMPORARY ZEN STYLE

NEUTRAL COLORS. Combinations of blacks, pure whites, and soft grays. These may be mixed with warmer neutrals, such as creams, taupes, and earthy browns.

SMOOTH CABINETRY. Plain-fronted cabinets crafted of fine-grain and exotic woods, such as teak, bird's-eye maple, and black walnut, in natural finishes.

CONTEMPORARY FIXTURES. Sleek faucets with simple curves and clean lines.

VISUAL BALANCE. Symmetrical arrangements of fixtures and cabinetry so visual weight appears evenly spread throughout the room.

For more information on **Asian style**, visit *HGTV.com/designstyles*

FENG SHUI

To bring a Zen feel to your bath—similar to the one shown on pages 98–101—include a few *Feng Shui* products and principles.

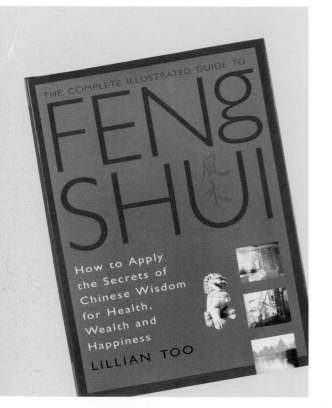

READ ALL ABOUT IT *Feng Shui,* which means "wind and water," dates back 4,000 years when ancient Chinese philosophers encouraged Asian people to live in harmony with the environment in order to reduce stress and feel content. Today this philosophy of creating balance is taking root in the West. To learn more about *Feng Shui,* visit your local library or bookstore and check out a book, such as the one *above,* on the principles of *Feng Shui* design.

THE FIVE ELEMENTS Bringing the elements of *Feng Shui* design into your home can be as easy as purchasing a set of candles. The candles *below* represent the five necessary elements of *Feng Shui* design: water, earth, fire, wood, and metal. Ancient Chinese philosophers believe the balance of these elements affects one's attitude. You can purchase *Feng Shui* candles at most bed and bath shops, at many home accessory stores, on the Internet, and from home decorating catalogs.

THE POWER OF NATURE Bring a touch of natural Asian beauty into your home with a beautiful blooming orchid *below*. The earliest written evidence of orchids dates back to circa 700 B.C. in Chinese and Japanese drawings and literature. At that time orchids were used as herbs and cures for many maladies. The simple beauty of the flower complements the uncluttered beauty of Zen baths, as do stalks of bamboo and pots of tall grasses. You can purchase live orchids from a florist or garden center, on the Internet, and from floral catalogs.

PAMPERED BODY

ZEN BATHS LIKE the one featured on pages 98-101 exude serenity through neutral colors and smooth finishes that calm and relax the spirit. Although a plethora of accessories doesn't fit the design scheme, you can indulge your senses with thick Egyptian cotton towels and heavy terry robes stored on heated bars, as well as with soothing soaps, bath oils, and scented candles.

THE SOUND OF *FENG SHUI* *Feng Shui* music also encourages relaxation and comfort in hopes of bringing more balance to your life. A large variety of CDs *right* and tapes is available from music shops and on the Internet. Play them in the bath to sooth and calm yourself as you prepare for the day or night.

COLOR
HAPPY

Wake up to good hues every day when you lavish your bath with colors sure to make you smile.

Paint and fabric prove their "wow" power as they punch up this bathroom with loads of glorious color.

Colors from the bathroom continue to the built-in storage in the hallway *right*. In the bath striped fabric used for the shower curtain border embellishes hanging towels.

YOUR BATH DOESN'T HAVE TO BE new to present a happier face to the world. Add color to your new or old bath to jazz up the atmosphere and give it (and you) a sunny attitude—no matter the weather. This little bath in an older home shows the possibilities of a lively color palette.

MAGIC MIX

If you have more than one favorite color, you may be able to include them all in the bathroom. (See page 108 to learn more about successfully incorporating several colors in one space.) This bath shoves convention out the door and invites in orange, yellow, green, purple, and red without missing a beat. White fixtures make the colors pop.

BEFORE

Before the makeover this modestly sized bathroom *left* looked a little lackluster; the shower curtain produced the only bit of understated color.

One of the least expensive ways to bring color into the bathroom is with paint. Use paint to brighten a small, dark bath and to highlight architectural features. For painted surfaces that can stand up to moisture and offer easy cleaning, select semi-gloss latex paint. In this bathroom a bold swath of orange-red draws attention to the arch above the bathtub niche. On the remaining walls painted horizontal stripes, in a series of progressive shades of green, offer an unexpected element and an opportunity for more color. You can also use paint to refresh cabinetry or even a bathtub. Built-in storage just outside this bathroom takes a playful turn with various shades of green stacking up on the drawer fronts with two more shades of green highlighting an upper door. (For more on using paint in the bath, turn to page 128.)

FASHIONABLE FABRIC

Fabric is another fast and practical way to introduce color and pattern into a bath. Shower curtains, window treatments, sink

Coordinating fabrics *above* provide eye-popping color for a small bath.

skirts, and bath mats are just a few of the elements that allow you to use fabric.

In this bathroom the new glass-block window in the shower didn't need a window treatment, but the other fabric options mentioned come into play. For the shower a whimsical flower-motif fabric pairs with a stripe to bring in a bundle of color. Dark apple green-color fabric combines with the same stripe used for the shower curtain to fashion a skirt for the wall-hung sink. The skirt attaches with hook-and-loop tape and creates hidden storage beneath the sink. (Above the sink the existing medicine cabinet dresses up with the addition of a stenciled border of frosted-glass spray paint.) Towels earn their stripes with an embellishment of the same border fabric used on the skirt and shower curtain. More towels stitched together form a multistripe bath mat for the floor. (To learn how to make the shower curtain, the sink skirt, and the bath mat, turn to pages 160–167.)

Details, such as a fabric-lined basket, sprinkle more color around the room. To learn more about bringing color into the bath, turn the page.

Adding a fabric skirt to a pedestal sink softens the look of this utilitarian element and creates hidden storage underneath *top*. (To learn how to make a sink skirt, turn to page 166.)

Stitch together a collection of colorful towels to make this comfy bath mat *above*, then embroider the flowers for additional panache. (To learn how to make this bath mat, turn to page 164.)

CREATIVE COLOR

THESE ARE A FEW of the many ways you can bring stylish color into your bathroom.

FABRIC

RUGS

PAINT FOR THE WALLS, the vanity, the countertop, and even the bathtub and toilet (see pages 132–133)

TOWELS *right*

ARTWORK AND ACCESSORIES, such as toothbrush and tissue holders

DRAWER AND DOOR PULLS

GLASS SHADES for lighting fixtures

STRIPE A WALL

TO CREATE STRIPED WALLS in your bathroom, purchase paints in colors you like. These horizontal stripes use various shades of green, starting with the darkest green as the bottom stripe and progressing to the lightest shade of green at the top.

Paint the entire wall the lightest shade; let dry. Measure and mark off the height of the stripes using a

carpenter's level and a pencil. (These stripes measure about 25 inches high. The height selected matches the height of the arch above the bathtub.) Tape off alternating stripes with low-tack painter's tape and paint the stripes the desired color. Immediately remove the tape; let the paint dry. Tape off the remaining alternating stripes and paint those the desired color. Remove the tape; let dry.

EMBELLISH A MIRROR

YOU CAN ADD A DESIGN to a plain mirror using a stencil and frosted-glass spray paint, as shown *below*. Frosted-glass spray paint is fairly durable and will stand up to light cleaning, but it isn't as permanent as personalizing a mirror with etching cream.

TO ETCH A MIRROR, purchase etching cream from a crafts or art supply store. You will also need clear adhesive-back vinyl, a design to stencil or trace, scissors, a crafts knife, latex gloves and goggles, a foam brush or an artist's brush, and a clean lint-free rag.

LEAVE THE BACKING ON the clear vinyl and trace the desired design onto the front of the vinyl. Cut away excess vinyl with the scissors; then pull away a small portion of the backing and position the vinyl design on the mirror in the desired location. Continue to pull away the backing paper, adhering the vinyl to the clean glass and working out bubbles.

USE A CRAFTS KNIFE to cut away the design outlines. Remove the vinyl in areas where you want to apply the etching cream. Wear latex gloves and goggles and open a window for ventilation. Stir the cream. Use a foam brush or an artist's brush to thickly and evenly apply etching cream within the cutouts of the vinyl stencil. (Follow the manufacturer's suggestions for application and allow the cream to set for the prescribed time.) Rinse away the cream with water, remove the vinyl, and polish the glass with a clean lint-free rag.

COLOR IN THE BATH

The bath on pages 104–107 proves there is no need to settle for predictable white. You have 10 million color choices, so here's help finding a color scheme you'll love.

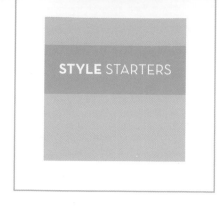

SOFT AND SUBDUED Select low-intensity versions of hues for a softness that's easy to live with. For instance pick gold instead of canary yellow or raspberry rather than bright red. Muted gray-greens make this master bathroom *below* a tranquil oasis.

MIDDLE OF THE ROAD Bring your bathroom to life and prevent it from looking stiff by varying the intensity of the colors. Whether you choose intense or low-intensity versions of your color palette, add a bit of the opposite into the room, such as with a rug. This Zenlike retreat *above* mixes the stronger intensities of green slate flooring and cherry wood with butter-yellow walls to provide a softer diversion. To learn more about this bathroom, turn to page 138.

BRIGHT AND LOVELY Want your room to make a bold statement? Select intense colors, such as the shower curtain *above* and featured in the bath on pages 104–107. Choose the purest shades of the colors in your trio (true blue instead of navy, for example). Fresh, vivid colors will brighten your bathroom and show off your spunky personality.

COLOR CHOICES

COLOR IS WHERE everything starts in redoing your bathroom, from purchasing paint to finding just the right towels and accessories. Before you can decorate your bathroom, choose a color palette.

INSPIRATIONAL APPROACH. Interior designers often start the planning process with an inspirational piece in hand. It may be the fabric you want to use for a shower curtain or sink skirt, or it might be a piece of artwork you plan to display in the bathroom. From your inspirational piece, pull out a primary, secondary, and accent color, and voilá—you have a color palette. Choosing colors this way eliminates worries about whether certain colors match or clash.

FOOLPROOF FORMULA. If you are uncertain how big each dose of color should be, use a 60-30-10 formula as a foolproof guide. According to the formula, a predominant color should cover 60 percent of the room (usually the painted walls or possibly the majority of the cabinets). A secondary color covers 30 percent (window treatments, upholstery, rugs), while accent colors account for the remaining 10 percent (artwork, hand towels, and pottery). Although you don't need to be specific about these percentages, this formula can help you decide how much of each color is adequate.

For more ideas on **using color in your bath**, visit *HGTV.com/color*

KID
FABULOUS

Decorate a new or existing bathroom to please the kids in your house or the kid in you.

Separate vanities make this bathroom ideal for children to share. Painting the walls different colors to suit each child's personality helps identify whose vanity is whose.

KIDS JUST WANT TO HAVE FUN,
so why not make your children's bathroom
as exuberant as they are? See how you can
artfully use a combination of hip features
and cool colors to parlay playfulness into
a shared bath at your house.

COLORING LESSONS

When you look back and remember how
thrilled you were with a new box of crayons,
you can relate to why a child loves a
colorful room. You can decorate a bath
with your child's favorite color, combining
various shades of the same hue with an
accent color or two. Or take a cue from
this shared bath and paint every wall a
different color to satisfy siblings with
distinctive opinions. (For tips on selecting
colors, turn to page 108.) The walls in this
bath sport bright orange, hot pink, and
lime green. (To achieve this look at home
and create crisp edges where wall colors
meet in the corners, paint one wall in the
desired color; let dry. Then tape off each
long edge of the painted wall with low-tack
painter's tape; paint the abutting walls right
up to the tape.)

   To bolster the sense of vivaciousness, add
towels in a rainbow of colors as well as throw

Invest in a colorful shower curtain
and pump up an ordinary fiberglass
shower interior inexpensively with
clear plastic bottles. Fill the bottles
with multicolor shampoos, soaps,
and bath oil.

KID STYLE

COLOR. Stick with solids and patterns that will grow with your
child. (Popular cartoon characters and other special motifs are
soon yesterday's news.) Include plenty of fun colors in the form
of painted walls and vanities, rugs, towels, and accessories.

FUNKY ATTITUDE. Add some unexpected features, such as CD
covers as artwork or a hockey stick standing in as a shower curtain rod.

STORAGE. Kids are more likely to pick up when storage containers
are out in the open. Incorporate open shelves so they can display
personal items and use some of the space to hold baskets for
towels and toiletries. Keep a hamper in the bath for laundry.

rugs in different hues. This bathroom also invites a mix of accessories, such as small colorful boxes, clear plastic bottles filled with brightly colored soaps and shampoos, fresh flowers, and a bright green shower curtain.

NEW VIEWS

You can also provide ways for your children to personalize the bathroom with photographs and philosophy. Ideas in this bathroom make it easy for them to do both. Beside one vanity the wall becomes a photo gallery with the addition of a display kit (available through catalogs and online sources); it features wire snaked through metal holders that screw into the walls. Metal clips hold photos and other lightweight memorabilia anywhere along the wire.

You can use another wall to overcome the communication gap with a message board. For a hip, industrial look, surface portions of a wall with sheet metal, allowing some of the wall color to show, then let the kids use magnetic-backed words and images to speak their minds. (For instructions to duplicate the metal wall, see "Magnetic Messages," *opposite far right*.)

For still more kid-friendly bath ideas, turn the page.

Towels and area rugs *left* let you pull various colors anywhere in the room. Don't worry about matching accessories to the wall color exactly; accessories that are lighter or darker than the paint create visual variety.

This wire photo display *above* is available in kit form through catalogs and online, but you could get a similar look by threading wire through eyehooks screwed into the wall. Use metal clips to attach photographs along the wire.

MAGNETIC MESSAGES

TO MAKE THIS FUN and funky metal wall for posting magnetic messages and images, purchase 24×36-inch sheets of galvanized metal. (You can find these at a home center.) Starting in one corner of the bath wall, use double-stick tape to temporarily adhere the sheets to the wall. Stagger and overlap the sheets as desired; experiment with the total arrangement until you achieve a look and coverage you like. (By overlapping the sheets, you never have to cut any to a different size.)

When the sheets are arranged as you like them, slip washers over screws, such as drywall screws, that have a tip sharp enough to penetrate the metal. Use an electric screwdriver to drive the screws into each corner of all the metal sheets. Arrange magnetic-backed words and images on the sheets as you wish.

SAFE KIDS

NEVER LEAVE SMALL CHILDREN alone in a bathroom, and no matter the age of your kids, incorporate these safety features and rules in the bathroom they use:

GROUND FAULT CIRCUIT INTERRUPTER (GFCI). This device protects against electrical shock by shutting off the flow of electricity to an outlet when an atypical discharge is detected, such as a hair dryer being dropped into a water-filled sink.

NONSLIP SURFACES. The bathroom floor and surfaces inside the tub and shower should include materials that are slip-resistant. Purchase bath mats and rugs with nonslip backings; step stools should feature slip-resistant caps on the feet.

HOT WATER CONTROLS. Equip the sinks, shower, and bathtub with faucets outfitted with anti-scald or pressure-balanced devices. (A plumber can advise you.) Or turn down the hot-water heater to 120 degrees to avoid scalding.

NO-GLASS ZONE. Designate the bathroom as an area off-limits to glass cups or containers. Instead purchase plastic cups for rinsing mouths and acrylic holders for storing cotton balls and other supplies.

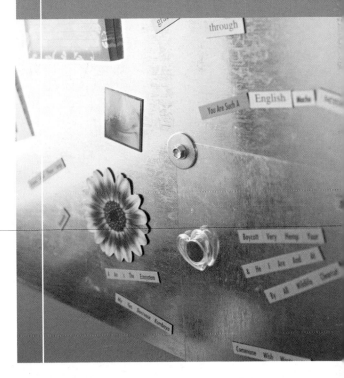

KID STUFF

If you want to create a fun, colorful kids' bath like the one shown on pages 110–113, playful products such as these can help you pull it together.

CLEAN GETAWAY To display and dispense colorful liquid soaps and lotions, purchase clear container pumps *above*.

LIGHTS, CAMERA, ACTION Cast a cool light on the bathroom using a fixture with a hip, colorful shade. The one *above* features a shiny chrome base and a hot pink shade with a punched design. Pair the fixture on a vanity countertop with playful frames to hold photos of family and friends.

To see more **children's spaces** plus dozens of bathrooms in a variety of styles, visit *HGTV.com/designstyles*

TIME'S UP Whether your kids are getting ready for school or they have a time limit for their turn in the bathroom, include a clock to help them keep track. This one *below* comes in hot pink with a striped face.

HOLD EVERYTHING A linen closet isn't the only place to store towels and soaps. This lime green-color canvas tower *above* lets you stack towels and other items in one compact corner on top of a countertop. Save the beige towels for Grandma and Grandpa and stock up on jazzy, colorful ones for the kids.

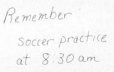

Remember
soccer practice
at 8:30 am

Love,
Mom

FISHY NEWS Suspend a shower curtain from fun fish-shaped rings *right*, or other motifs kids love. Use a shapely message clip for posting reminders and other notes.

Antique robe hooks and a tapestry lend classical style to the bathtub alcove. Whenever you bring antiques into a wet bathroom environment, keep in mind that the moisture eventually could deteriorate the finish or material. Bring in only those pieces you can part with. French doors at one end of this bath open to a secluded patio where the owner and friends often enjoy a cup of coffee.

CLASSICAL ELEGANCE

Outfit a bath with an antique table, seating, and an area rug and you gain a setting with the feel of a formal sitting room.

EMBRACE YOUR APPRECIATION of antiques and artifacts by using some of your loveliest pieces, typically reserved for a formal, refined sitting room, to create an elegant bathroom. One caveat: You may want to use less valuable reproductions rather than authentic antiques. In a wet bathroom environment, stained or painted wood, upholstery, tapestries, and rugs could all eventually suffer water damage. In this bathroom a generous space accommodates reproduction and antique accessories and furnishings.

VANITY FOCAL POINT

Make the vanity a lovely focal point that suits fine, classic antiques or reproductions by giving it a beautiful finish and furniture details. This extra-long vanity *left* features three cabinet sections—one center cabinet is pulled forward for variety—and intricately adorned panels and borders. Claw feet, a marble top, and a glazed ivory finish give it the appeal of a long sideboard.

Crown the vanity area with a formal mirror framed as if it were fine artwork. This vanity boasts an extra-large mirror with an ornate gilded frame.

FURNISHED FLAIR

An important component of creating a classically elegant bathroom is antique or reproduction furnishings. Of course no

Fabric lighting sconces embrace a gilt-framed mirror to make the vanity wall *left* an artful focal point. Fresh flowers in a white antique pitcher pair with a filigree clock and framed artwork to accessorize the vanity as if it were a dining room sideboard.

When the owner wants to further enhance the living room illusion of this bathroom, a solid faux-marble door can be closed to conceal the shower *opposite*. An upholstered chair provides the kind of comfortable seating found in an elegant sitting room.

living room seating area comes together without a fabulous rug to ground the grouping. This bathroom arrangement begins with an antique carpet, previously used in the owner's dining room. The rug rests under an antique wooden table that anchors the room and serves as a countertop for toiletries and other needs.

FINISHING TOUCHES

Infuse your bathroom with good general lighting that fits the new theme by trading the standard bathroom lighting fixture for a chandelier. In this bathroom a grand crystal and iron rendition hanging above the long console table offers formal living room flair.

Treat walls as you would a living room, finishing them with elegant

coverings or a special faux paint treatment. The walls in this bathroom feature a faux-marble finish, applied using sweeping strokes of rusty-peach glaze on a cream-color foundation. To complement the walls, the painted woodwork portrays a subtle faux-maple wood grain.

Finally accessorize with treasures you find in antique stores and at estate auctions (or flea markets for more affordable flair). The accessories throughout this bath, such as the matched pair of hurricane pedestal lanterns on the console table and the tapestry hanging in the bathtub alcove, were found during various shopping forays for antiques.

For more ideas to help you furnish a classically elegant bath, turn the page.

THE WELL-FURNISHED BATH

One way to create a classically elegant bath, such as the one on pages 116–119, is to furnish the space much as you would a formal living room. Use these ideas to inspire your own beautifully furnished bath.

PETITE ADDITION Tuck small, ornate tables or plant stands around the room to hold towels, toiletries, or a vibrant bouquet of fresh flowers. If the room gets steamy, protect stained wood pieces with a polyurethane finish. This low table *above* has been placed beside the bathtub to hold reading material and a beverage.

CLASSIC CABINETRY Choose cabinetry with furniturelike lines and details such as feet and reproduction hardware. Or retrofit an antique sideboard or dresser to hold a sink. This mahogany cabinet *below* looks like an antique but is a reproduction outfitted with a sink and sconces.

ART AND COMFORT Bring in cushy upholstered chairs, ottomans, and stools, such as the one *left* to enhance the feel of a fine living room. In the same vein, hang framed prints and position good-looking racks, shelves, and small cabinets above toilets, between windows, over doors, or on bare walls. Introduce unpredictable, refined accessories, such as the mirrored bamboo case on this cosmetics counter.

SINK STYLE Accessorize beyond the standard bathroom fare, introducing specialty fixtures and fittings with finely crafted details. This hand-painted porcelain sink *right* is reminiscent of a beautiful antique bowl. Even the ceramic handles flanking the faucet are hand-painted.

SEASIDE SOOTHER

An all-white bath is clean and bright but too stark. Borrow beauty from the beach and you'll never tire of your retreat.

Soft green paint on the walls instantly transforms this formerly all-white master bathroom from cold to charismatic beach cottage style. Plain mirrors perk up with the addition of white-painted frames fashioned from inexpensive molding. An empty space in the middle of the room inspired designer Kristan Cunningham to add a comfortable cushioned bench for that area—a great spot for sitting and undressing or toweling off. (For more ideas on adding comfort to your bathroom, turn to page 126.)

WHETHER YOUR BATHROOM is in a new or existing home, it can suffer from the same "too much white" syndrome and have an unattractive jumble of towels hanging on one wall, as this bath did. Located in a new home, this spacious master bathroom houses a big whirlpool tub and a separate shower. But its all-white cabinetry and plain white walls showed little personality.

Enter the *Design on a Dime* team: Designer Kristan Cunningham, working with teammates Spencer Anderson and Dave Sheinkopf, added color to the walls, stylish details, a custom-built shelf for the towels, and a comfortable place to sit in the middle of the room. The result is a soothing retreat with details evocative of a beach cottage. Remedy a similar dilemma at your house by inviting in charming beach-cottage style.

Before the bathroom offered great amenities but was dressed in all white *below.*

BEFORE

A chaotic assembly of towels on one wall (see the Before photo *below*) yielded to this crisp, custom-built shelf *right*. Fresh rolled towels or decorative accessories can adorn the shelf; towels hang-dry on the rod. If the owners prefer to keep the center of the bathroom open, the upholstered bench can be easily relocated beneath the towel rack.

AHH, SPA

Shaping your own seaside spa begins with soft color on the walls to tone down the harshness of the white. Adding wall color also allows the white vanities and tub surround to stand out as visual bonuses, rather than disappearing into the walls. In this room the wall color, reminiscent of pale green sea glass, establishes the oceanside atmosphere. (Sea glass is the remnants of colored glass vessels—often vintage bottles and jars—smoothed and shaped over a long period of time by the natural forces of the sea and sand.) (To learn which other colors work with this relaxed decorating style, see "Beach Cottage Style," page 124.)

NEW DIMENSION

Although painting your bathroom walls will help the vanities and tub to visually hold their own, the large mirrors that typically hang above the vanities can

Kristan replaced plain recessed fixtures above the vanities with fashionable pendant fixtures *above*. Each shade and light kit cost just $38, resulting in more stylish lighting for little expense.

FRAME A MIRROR

LARGE MIRRORS make a bathroom seem larger and brighter, but the unadorned glass can also appear as an afterthought. Customize the mirrors in your new or existing bath by adding a wood frame, as Kristan did:

MEASURE the height and length of the mirror (considering whether the frame will slightly overlap the mirror or wrap around the outside).

START WITH 1× LUMBER in the desired width or use molding.

USE A CIRCULAR SAW or a table saw to cut the frame pieces—two sides and pieces for the top and bottom—to the desired lengths.

USE A MITER BOX and a backsaw or a compound mitersaw to miter the ends of the frame pieces.

PAINT or stain the pieces; let dry.

SECURE THE FRAME around the mirror. You can either 1) finish-nail the frame pieces together and use construction adhesive to glue the frame to the wall around the mirror (don't glue the frame to the mirror because the glue will be visible in the mirror), or 2) leave the pieces separate and put them into place one-by-one around the mirror. Use finishing nails to secure the frame to the wall. Wherever possible drive the nails into wall studs for added security. Fill the nail holes with wood filler; let dry. Touch up the filled spots with paint.

appear lackluster. For some style oomph, frame the mirror with wood or tile. Kristan opted for white-painted molding to give the mirrors dimension without disrupting the soothing setting. (For information on framing a mirror with wood, see "Frame a Mirror" *left*. To learn how to frame a mirror with tile, turn to page 158.)

To make your all-white bathroom warmer and more inviting, introduce accessories, plants, and upgraded lighting. Special touches in this bathroom include candles, Roman shades, beach-theme artwork, a bamboo plant (an unexpected Asian accent that complements the new casual style), and pendant fixtures with swirling white-on-white glass shades hanging from black stems for a subtle, cottage-style lighting accent.

SHELF ASSURANCE

Dave makes his own contribution to the soothing surroundings by organizing the clutter of towels with a long shelf equipped with a hanging rod and pegs. Alternatively you can purchase a shelf and add beaded board to the sides to gain a beachside cottage connection. Use the shelf for clean rolled towels and the hanging rod or pegs for air-drying towels.

COTTAGE BENCH

Enhance the beach cottage theme by making your bath more comfortable with

For more information on **cottage style**, visit HGTV.com/designstyles

BEACH COTTAGE STYLE

SOFT COLOR associated with the beach: ocean blue or green, sky blue, sandy beige, or sea glass green. Remaining touches of crisp white play up the cottage angle.

BASKETS OF SEASHELLS or artwork depicting seashells or other beach-related scenes.

CABANA-STRIPE FABRICS or soft white-color canvas.

TERRY CLOTH-COVERED CUSHIONS or pillows; choose white for an airy atmosphere.

upholstered seating. Spencer lends portable comfort to this bath by constructing a bench seat that can be easily moved to other areas of the bath, as shown on page 123. Shelves in the base and a terry cloth-covered cushioned top make this piece pretty and functional. Choosing a shade of green slightly darker than the walls sets the bench apart without jarring the soothing surroundings. (To make your own bench, see "Cushion a Bench" *opposite*.)

For more ideas on increasing the comfort of your bathroom, turn the page.

CUSHION A BENCH

IF YOU DON'T have the skills or the time to build your own bench base, purchase one from a home center or discount store. (A bench with a flip-up lid will provide additional storage for towels and toiletries.) Prime and paint the bench as desired; let dry. Cushion the bench by laying a piece of upholstery foam onto the seat. Purchase 4-inch-thick foam for added padding or use a double layer of 2-inch-thick foam. Wrap the foam in acrylic batting, pulling the batting around the sides of the foam and to the bottom of the bench seat. Lay a piece of terry cloth (or other absorbent fabric) on top of the batting as shown *below left*. Pull the ends of the batting and fabric layers underneath the seat and staple the edges to the bottom of the seat *below right*.

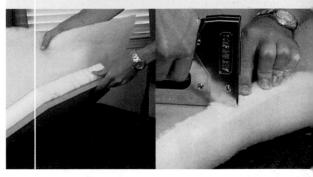

Absorbent terry cloth is practical for the bench top *above left*. Purchase terry cloth by the bolt or buy towels and use them as yardage.

An existing stool garnered a makeover with black paint for the base and a white terry cloth cover *above right*. (To learn how to add fabric to a cushion, see "Cushion a Bench" *above*.)

Accessories, such as a shelf to hold a container of sea sponges and a vase of bamboo, make the tub area *left* inviting. Roman shades soften the look of basic blinds.

125

COMFORT PLUS

Comfort comes in many forms. The bathroom shown on pages 122–125 makes room for comfort with cushioned seating, easy-access storage, and other amenities. Make your bathroom more hospitable with these soothing additions.

SITTING PRETTY Even a small bathroom may have room for a chair so you can sit down to take off your shoes. This chair *above* can move close to the tub or shower and double as a place to set your towel and other bath-time needs.

COUNTER POINTS Standing and stooping over to apply makeup or put in your contacts doesn't make for a comfortable beginning to the day. Carve out a space in your new or existing bathroom for a lower countertop and a stool or chair as shown *below*. Equip your counter with a magnified mirror and storage for the necessities you use for your morning and evening routines.

SHINE ON Adequate lighting is often an afterthought but is an important consideration for making your bathroom inviting and comfortably functional. This three-fixture light *below* illuminates a mirror and vanity underneath. (To learn more about lighting your bathroom, turn to page 30.)

WARM FLOORS

CREATE COMFORT UNDERFOOT by taking the chill off stone and tile floors. Install a radiant heating system below new flooring in a new or existing bathroom. These heating systems not only warm the floor but also increase the overall temperature of the room, often eliminating the need for additional heaters.

Radiant heating systems typically have a network of electrical heating cables or hot water-filled tubes installed between the subfloor and finish floor. Most systems can be installed across the entire floor or confined to a specific area, such as the space in front of a vanity or tub. Like other heating systems, radiant heating is controlled by a thermostat that can be turned on or off, up or down.

You can either install a radiant heating system yourself—they are available at most home centers—or hire a flooring professional to install the system for you. Materials and installation typically cost $4 to $6 per square foot.

For more information on flooring, turn to page 44.

STORAGE AND MORE A vanity with an open shelf, such as the one *right*, is an ideal place for storing stacks of thick, absorbent towels. Providing a sink-in, soft rug in front of the vanity offers comfort underfoot while you brush your teeth and comb your hair.

SIGNATURE PAINT

Paint personality into your bath with decorative finishes and handcrafted designs.

A painted and glazed finish makes the armoire *opposite* look like an antique. Acrylic panels on the smaller doors reveal what the cabinet holds. A mirror covers the larger door, making interior neatness less of an issue.

YOU DON'T HAVE TO SPEND a fortune to pack your bath with the personality of a fine old European hotel. Easy-to-do decorative paint finishes can take your bath back to an earlier time.

Instead of choosing built-in cabinets for the vanities and storage centers, furnish the room with affordable freestanding pieces reminiscent of times past. Then paint on finishes and details that make each piece a study in old-fashioned individuality. Here two new pieces—a freestanding storage armoire *opposite* and a narrow dresser shown on page 131—sport creamy painted and glazed finishes that appear timeworn.

Spread the vintage illusion to the walls with a two-tone stippling technique (see "Wow Walls" on page 131) and to mirror frames and sconces with a crackle paint finish (see "Crackle Cover" on page 132). For more period authenticity, choose a pedestal sink similar to the one *opposite* and wood planks or stone or stone-look tiles for the floor.

COLOR CONNECTION

Use color as a visual connector for a totally painted room, slightly varying the shades between pieces and surfaces to create the appearance of aging paint and pieces added over time. This bath sports creamy shades as well as various greens. Faded accents, such as floral arrangements of purple-painted irises on the dresser—seen in the armoire mirror *opposite*—enliven the soft, casual color scheme.

Sconces with a crackle finish came from a local lighting store. The fixtures complement the crackle finish on the mirror. (For instructions on painting a crackle finish, see page 132.)

This bath, designed as a tranquil getaway for Mom, features a pedestal sink, two freestanding cabinets, and a combination tub and shower. The toilet is tucked away next to the large armoire.

DISTRESSED DRESSER

TO MAKE A DRESSER look centuries old, remove the drawers and lightly sand each component. Wipe the pieces clean with a tack cloth. Prime all the surfaces; let dry. Next base-coat the piece with dark taupe-color latex paint, followed by a top coat of cream-color latex paint, allowing each color to dry between coats. Lightly sand the edges and corners of the cream-color paint, letting some of the deeper taupe base coat show through to create the appearance of wear. Clean off the sanding dust with a tack cloth. For more decorative appeal, paint on additional embellishments either freehand or using stencils; let dry. To protect the distressed finish, coat each piece once again with polyacrylic; let dry. Reassemble the piece.

For more ways to instill painted style in your bathroom, turn the page.

WOW WALLS

CREATE TEXTURAL dots all over your walls, as shown in this bath *bottom left*, with a stippling brush. Base-coat the walls with a light-color flat- or eggshell-finish paint. Roll a glaze slightly darker than the base coat onto a 3- or 4-foot-square section of the wall. While the glaze is still wet, pounce a stippling brush *top left* in a tight pattern over the glaze. Repeat the procedure until all the walls are glazed. If necessary wipe the brush to remove any excess glaze that builds up on it. For a more pronounced pattern, vary the glaze and wall color by several shades.

ANTIQUED ARMOIRE

TO MAKE AN UNFINISHED HUTCH look like a treasured antique, such as the one featured on page 128, remove the drawers and doors and lightly sand each component. Wipe the pieces clean with a tack cloth. Prime all the surfaces; let dry. Apply two coats of cream-color latex enamel paint, letting the paint dry between coats. Next, using a clean, lint-free cloth, coat the pieces with a dark taupe- or coffee-color glaze and then wipe off any excess glaze with a second clean, lint-free cloth. Allow the remaining glaze to dry thoroughly. To protect the antiqued finish, coat each piece with polyacrylic; let dry. Reassemble the piece.

A long, narrow dresser brings style and storage to the wall across from the toilet. A distressed finish makes the piece look centuries old.

PAINTED STYLE

As proven on pages 128–131, you can fill your bath with style
using a few easy decorative painting techniques.

COUNTER COVER Give a dated laminate counter a fresh new
look and another year or two of use (depending on how frequently
the bath is used) with heavy-duty primer and floor paint. Clean the
counter surface as usual; let dry. Ask the paint store to tint a floor-
quality primer the same color as the base floor paint. Brush or roll
on the primer; let dry. Apply two coats of the floor paint; let dry.
Protect the painted counter with three or four coats of polyacrylic;
let the finish dry between coats. For more painted style, the
owners added a taupe-color diamond to each side of the sink and
then stenciled words onto the painted squares *left*. You can paint a
vinyl floor using the same products and techniques; just be sure to
lightly sand (to ensure paint adhesion) and thoroughly clean the
floor before applying the paint.

CRACKLE COVER Crackling is a fun, easy way to add personality to any
wood surface. Crackle medium is available at crafts stores and home
improvement centers. When applied between a base coat and a contrasting
top coat of latex paint—and allowed to cure for a set amount of time—it will
cause the top coat to split or crack so some of the base coat shows through.
Before beginning your project read the crackle manufacturer's directions
carefully; product curing times and application methods vary. Some brands
require two separate products, whereas others call for only one. If you have
never crackle-painted before, experiment with the technique on a piece of
primed foam-core board, using different color combinations, thicknesses of
crackle medium, and application tools (such as paintbrushes and sea sponges).
This mirror *right*, featured in the bath on pages 128–131, has a base coat of dark
taupe, followed by crackle medium and a top coat of cream-color paint.

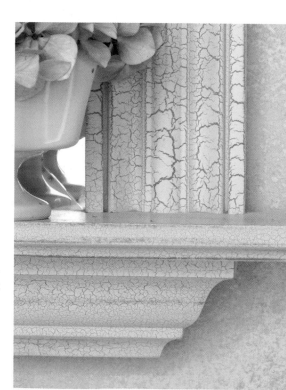

FIXTURE FINISH To bring color and whimsy to plain white bath fixtures, stencil (with stencils and stencil brushes) or paint on a freehand design (with artist's brushes) using permanent enamel paint. The paint is available at crafts stores and is durable enough to be wiped clean with a damp cloth. Grass green-color enamel paint adorns the toilet base and the floor tiles *below*. Latex paint in the same shade covers the walls.

RUG WORKS For a painterly approach with less permanence, add a stenciled design to a bamboo, sisal, or other natural fiber bath mat. A fern frond randomly scattered across the rug *above* creates a casual appearance. For best results use quality acrylic paint and a stencil brush to apply your design. You can use either premade stencils or cut your own from stencil plastic. (Use two stencils so you can flip the pattern without waiting for paint to dry on a single stencil.) Each of these products can be purchased at crafts stores. Before painting arrange paper cutouts the same size as your stencils on the mat in a pleasing pattern. Then replace the cutouts with a taped-on stencil and apply acrylic paint with a stencil brush using a pouncing motion. Repeat until all the designs are stenciled. Because of the texture of the rug, the painting will be uneven. Let the paint dry completely. Apply one or two coats of polyacrylic to the entire rug.

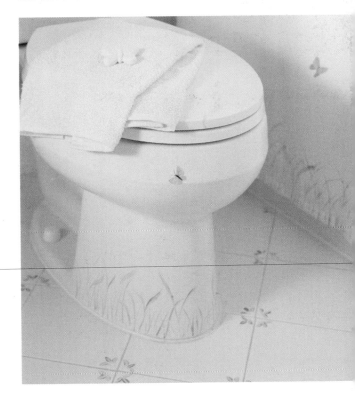

BETTER HALVES

Your powder room, or half bath, can be a minihaven with stylish personality as this space proves.

An ornately carved antique mirror has enough presence to stand out against the bold stripes in this powder room *opposite*. A simple white pedestal sink and a white toilet let the wall treatment shine.

IN A POWDER ROOM, or half bath—a bath equipped with only a sink and a toilet—the challenge is to make the room functional and interesting with minimal space and elements. This well-composed powder room edits the bath down to its essentials, yet still makes a compelling statement of personal style with traditional touches and bold accent color. Use its lessons to inspire your own half-bath treatment.

SMALL FAVORS

The small dimensions of a powder room (typically 6×4 or 5×5 feet) mean that the walls become especially important in the visual scheme. The good news is you may be able to budget for expensive fabrics, wallcoverings, and other features because you're dealing with small quantities. In this powder room bold stripes are the

star—a splurge created by a professional tole painter over a 10-day period. You can save money by creating the stripes yourself (see "Striped Style" *above*).

FIXTURE FINALES

If you decide to wrap your powder room in a dramatic wall treatment, select a lower-key vanity, sink, and toilet. Although the owner was fearless about adding stripes to this powder room, the traditional white pedestal sink and toilet let the stripes,

rather than the fixtures, take center stage.

On the other hand, if you opt for a quieter wall treatment, shop for a vanity and sink or a pedestal sink that will serve as the focal point. (For information on sinks and faucets, turn to page 70.) A low, ornate chest topped with an above-counter vessel sink is a good example of a vanity and sink that earn immediate attention in a small powder room.

For more ideas on giving your powder room panache, turn the page.

STRIPED STYLE

TO CREATE THE exciting striped treatment shown in this bath, follow these instructions:

BASE-COAT THE WALLS with pale khaki-color paint; let dry. Paint on red stripes slightly wider than the pale khaki stripes for interest. For crisp edges mask off the stripes with low-tack painter's tape. If you prefer a more casual appearance, draw vertical guidelines on the walls with a long carpenter's level and a colored pencil that matches the top coat stripes. Paint each stripe from the top down; let dry.

ACCENT the treatment with golden hand-painted stripes, using the technique noted above. The slightly wavy lines on the walls in this bath lend painterly appeal. If desired soften the stripes by brushing over the entire wall with glaze slightly tinted with black latex paint.

135

POWDER-ROOM POWER

Although it's likely the tiniest room in your house, your powder room can offer a big welcome to guests—as the space on pages 134–135 proves. Use these tips to make tight quarters lovely and luxurious.

FABULOUS FIXTURES Splurge on an eye-catching decorative faucet and handles, such as this white ceramic and chrome version on pages 134–135 and *below*. Because a powder room is used less often than other baths, you can concentrate on pleasing designs that may not be as practical for frequent use, such as an above-counter sink or this pedestal sink. (Pedestal sinks lack the storage of a vanity, but a powder room typically requires little storage.)

ART FOR A BATH Accessorize the powder room as you would other rooms, placing artwork on the wall. Choose one sizable piece or group several small items to make a display that reads as one unit. (But don't overwhelm the small space with accessories.) The bath shown on pages 134–135 and *above* includes this black- and gilt-framed mirror paired with a dresser for a furnished feel.

GREAT FOR YOUR GUESTS

Tend to your guests' comfort by anticipating their needs. Ensure privacy with window treatments and a good door lock. Provide flattering lighting, scented candles, soft towels, and fresh flowers *above* to welcome guests.

POWDER-ROOM STYLE

DECIDE ON THE FOCAL POINT. Potential attention-getters for a powder room are the walls, the vanity/sink, or, in a larger powder room, a chest of drawers and a mirror *opposite far left*. Spend the bulk of your budget on the focal-point feature you select.

BEGIN WITH ONE OR TWO ITEMS YOU LOVE. A wall covering, a fabric, or a cherished accessory can provide a good starting point around which to build your powder room design. For example an old-world scheme may begin with stone walls and floor tiles for a sense of timelessness and a silk window treatment fabric for color and softness.

LAYER ON ELEGANCE. Give your petite powder room a polished look by splurging on a few luxurious elements, such as expensive fabric or ornate sconces.

EXTEND THE FLOORING materials from adjoining spaces into the powder room to maintain continuity.

USE LARGE FLOOR TILES, resilient flooring with a large-scale pattern, or wide wood planks to eliminate distracting "seams" that can make a small floor look even smaller.

MAKE A SPACE LOOK LARGER by drawing attention to the height of the room with high-rise window treatments, crown molding, a painted border, or vertical stripes, such as the stripes in the powder room shown here and on pages 134-135. Mount valances on the wall above a window or on the ceiling. When the valance covers the molding, it fools the eye into seeing the window as larger.

AVOID TINY, BUSY PATTERNS, but make sure larger patterns aren't too disrupted by small walls and fixture placement.

KEEP STARK CONTRASTS—which stop the eye instead of allowing it to roam—to a minimum. For example paint the ceiling a tint of the wall color and choose complementary countertop and vanity colors. You can use dark or light hues in a powder room. Dark colors make the space feel cozy or more dramatic. Lighter shades make the room feel airy and spacious.

NATURAL OASIS

Experience the beauty of the outdoors every day in your bath with decor inspired by nature's bounty.

A bay window opens up the bath *opposite* to light and views and provides a spot for a roomy whirlpool tub. A cherry wood surround creates a visual tie between the tub and the vanities.

The curvy edges of the vanity countertops *above* replicate the gentle flow of ocean waves. The beefy edge treatment suggests mass, but only the edges are that deep; the solid surfacing is just $1/2$-inch thick.

FROM SMOOTH WOODS and stones to earthy textures and colors, natural materials entice all to come in, relax, and enjoy. This bath serves as a classic example of how you can warm a space with a variety of natural elements.

WOOD

To make your bath feel inviting and cocoonlike, choose cherry, maple, or mahogany cabinets stained a deep honey or rustic red tone. When combined with a warm stain color, the fine graining of these woods brings a sense of coziness to a room without overpowering the other decorative elements. The vanity cabinets in this bath are made from cherry wood stained a warm red tone to match the woodwork present throughout the rest of the home.

STONE AND TILE

Smooth, cool-to-the-touch stone and tile bring elegance and tactility to a room. When used on countertops and in bath and shower surrounds, both materials are functional and decorative, melding toughness and dependability with sleek sophistication. On the floor the materials look timeless and graceful and are virtually wear-proof. (For more information on stone and tile, see pages 44 and 96–97.) Here solid-surface counters resemble smooth limestone and provide interesting contrast against the colorful slate floor tiles.

COLOR AND TEXTURE

As with nature-inspired motifs, colors and textures commonly found in the outdoors are the perfect complement to a bath with terrestrial roots. Sage greens, faded blues,

MATCHING FORM TO FUNCTION

INDIVIDUAL ELEMENTS. When planning your bath, keep in mind that all elements in a space shared by two people don't need to match. In this bath each owner custom designed his or her own vanity base to match individual storage needs.

rustic reds, sunny yellows, and warm wood tones are natural companions of this style. Here warm cherry wood combines with faded blues, buttery yellows, soft grays, and sage greens to bring a sense of warmth and tranquility to the space. (For more information on selecting colors for your bath, see pages 108–109.)

NATURAL LIGHT AND VIEWS

Strengthen the connection between your bath and nature by maximizing views and sunlight. To accomplish that goal in this bath, the designer surrounded the tub with windows that maximize sunlight and views. Unobtrusive recessed lights sprinkled throughout the room enhance sunlight as necessary. To increase sunlight and views in your bath, install larger windows, add a skylight, and/or replace a solid exterior door with a glass model.

For additional ways to add natural elements to your bath, turn the page.

Curved vanities *left* help the couple share the space without getting in each other's way. For light with privacy, the shower has a glass-block wall inside, plus a door and window of etched glass. A heated slate floor and butter yellow walls add visual and functional warmth.

NATURAL STYLE

PAY HOMAGE to Mother Nature by filling your bath with elements found outdoors.

NATURAL SURFACES, such as wood floors, stained (not painted) cabinets, and stone or stone look-alike counters are mainstays.

A COLOR PALETTE derived from nature also creates the feeling of the great outdoors.

EARTH-INSPIRED TEXTURES that fit this style include natural-weave baskets, hand-hammered metals, and woven fabrics such as cotton, linen, and wool.

The vanity drawers *above left* follow the curve of the countertop. An electric outlet and a hole for a cord in the back of one drawer allow a hairdryer to be plugged in at all times. The shapely cabinet pulls are solid bronze with a brushed nickel finish.

Like the sink faucets, the tub filler *above right* features a high-arched spout that plays off the oval shape of the tub.

141

ODE TO NATURE

Capture the simple drama of a natural-style bath—like the one shown on pages 138–141—with decorative items that accentuate the elements of the earth.

FOCAL-POINT SINKS Bring visual excitement to your vanity top with a sink that resembles a freestanding bowl *left*. The simple shape is reminiscent of the days of wash basins and pitchers and is a perfect complement to a natural bath. A wall-mounted or high-arched faucet as shown *below left* also works well in this uncomplicated design scheme.

BOTANICAL TILES Give the backsplash, shower, and tub surround another connection to nature with natural stone tiles such as the slate featured on pages 138–141 or by adding a few decorative tiles that accentuate a botanical theme as this grouping *right* does.

SLEEK HANDLES Choose simple hardware that complements the clean lines of the style. For added design dash mount handles at different angles. Although these handles *below* were custom-made from aluminum, mahogany, and beech, you can find similar stainless-steel varieties at home centers.

LIVE PLANTS Bring color and life into your bath with a few potted plants *above*. Choose houseplants that thrive in warm, moist conditions and in the level of natural light found in your bath.

NATURAL REFLECTION If the only place you can find to put a window—a necessity in a natural-style bath—is directly above the sink, combine a window and mirror as shown *right*. Here a circular mirror mounted on metal rods hangs from the ceiling in front of an existing window.

143

VINTAGE MIX

Discover the attractive possibilities when elegant designs from several past eras coexist with modern luxury amenities.

Although the Roman shade in the bath alcove features a crisp contemporary fabric, gold tassel fringe makes a connection to the past. The silver candelabra and the vintage-style faucet—both on the tub ledge—further the link to yesteryear.

Though the hutchlike cabinet between the sinks is traditionally styled, the aged finish allows the piece to partner comfortably with a pair of crisp white farmhouse-style console sinks. Mirrors framed in stonelike tiles feature arched tops as a reference to the architecture of older homes.

IF YOU DESIRE A BATH lavished in elegant old designs, you may find that you appreciate elements from more than one time period. The good news is that a great-looking bathroom doesn't have to be purely from one era. This beautiful master bathroom, for example, shows how it's possible to welcome Victorian, 1920s farmhouse, and other vintage designs into one space.

VINTAGE DECISIONS

The options for creating a blended vintage look are practically limitless, so you'll first need to discover which time periods capture your interest. Look through current and vintage books and magazines to view some style options and visit plumbing showrooms as well as designer showhouses for ideas. Once you determine which designs capture your fancy, study the architectural characteristics of your home and allow what you find to inspire other design decisions.

VINTAGE STYLE

ENCOMPASSING A BROAD RANGE OF ERAS, including Victorian and 1920s farmhouse, this bath mixes vintages with ease. So can you. Here are a few of the elements to consider:

SINK OPTIONS. Commode-style with legs, pedestal, wall-hung, or antique chest turned-vanity.

FLOORING. Wood planks or strips, mosaic tiles, stone with chattered edges.

BACKSPLASHES AND WAINSCOTING. Mosaic tiles, subway tiles, beaded board.

FAUCETS. Gooseneck, cross handles.

FABRICS. Toile, ticking, and reproduction motifs.

COLORS. Depend on a neutral backdrop to tie together various vintages. Accent with colors you love from rich jewel tones to softer greens, reds, or blues.

Above the tub, a television sets back unobtrusively in a niche. A bolt holds the TV in place, and wiring runs into the adjoining master bedroom to avoid the possibility of electrical shock.

For example in this bathroom the floor and wainscoting are surfaced with tiles hand-painted with selected shades of beige and cream. The resulting aged finish mimics tiles original to the house. A complementary beige color continues to the painted portions of the walls to keep the look subtle and uninterrupted. It's this neutral backdrop that sets the stage for introducing pieces from many eras into one bathroom.

This house also features arched passageways, which repeat in the mirrors on page 145 and above the alcoves for the bathtub (see page 144) and the shower *right*. Although the arches make the connection to the past, the large tub and spacious shower with two showerheads provide contemporary comfort. Colonial sconces on each side of the mirrors and an ornate Victorian-style chandelier *above right*—each of which looks like a candlelit fixture—team with recessed fixtures throughout the bath to provide lighting.

ANTIQUE AMENITIES

The vanities you select can go a long way to establishing a beautiful vintage focal point. Certain styles of pedestal sinks, wall-hung sinks, and sinks set into retrofitted antique chests can all communicate a different era that will work with other vintage elements. (For more information on sinks and faucets, turn to page 70.) In this bath handsome porcelain commode-style sinks on legs convey the simple style of a 1920s farmhouse. The faucets have a fancier flair more akin to Victorian style and dress up the sinks with a bit of finery. It's worth noting that although the faucets look old, they offer the reliability of new fixtures.

Partnering with the sinks (because they lack the storage offered by vanities) is a hutchlike cabinet with recessed panel drawer fronts and simple Shaker knobs.

OLD-FASHIONED ACCESSORIES

Finish your vintage-blend bath with decorative accessories with old-fashioned flavor, or bring in some true vintage treasures. You don't necessarily need a lot: This bathroom uses apothecary jars and a silver candelabra to complete the illusion.

For more ideas on giving your new or remodeled bath character from several time periods, turn the page.

The ornate black wrought-iron chandelier *top* draws the eye upward to highlight the high, peaked ceiling.

Because the beautiful arched entry to the shower becomes the focal point in this corner *above*, the contemporary sauna adjacent to it doesn't detract from the vintage atmosphere of the room.

BLENDED VINTAGE STATEMENTS

If the bath on pages 144–147 whetted your appetite for a bath that looks old using a combination of vintages, browse these tips and ideas for additional inspiration.

TURN FOR THE BETTER

UNMATCHED PORCELAIN faucet handles are common, affordable finds at flea markets and antiques stores. Here are three charming ways to give the handles new life in your blended vintage-style bath:

GET HOOKED. Mount the handles on a wall as robe and towel hooks.

FEEL THE PULL. Use the handles on drawers and cabinet doors for easy-to-grasp knobs.

TIE UP LOOSE ENDS. Use a pair of handles as curtain-rod finials or tiebacks to dress the window.

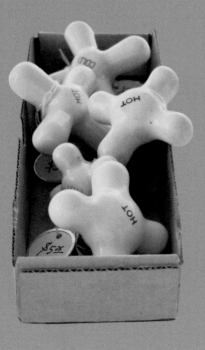

THE FURNISHED BATH Bring old furniture into your bath to provide comfort and to enhance the sense of another era. In this guest bathroom *above* the sconce, a side table, and an antique chair create an air of romance from the past.

ALL THE EXTRAS Well-chosen finishes, fixtures, and accessories will make your vintage bath complete. In this bathroom *above* beaded-board wainscoting provides the old-fashioned backdrop for a pedestal sink outfitted with a reproduction faucet with cross handles. Accessories, such as the magnifying mirror on the accordion extender and a shaving brush, enhance the sense of the past.

NEW BATH, OLD STYLE

GET THE LOOK OF YESTERYEAR with the following tips that bring some age and charm to a new bathroom:

COVER walls with beaded board *above* or wide-wood paneling (painted white or cream). Both make great neutral backdrops for welcoming various vintages.

SELECT faucets, tubs, and sinks with various vintage designs. Continue the theme with light fixtures that have antique styling.

LAY tile and flooring with antique-looking patterns and styles.

HANG a mirror (or mirrors) in an antique wood frame.

VISIT flea markets and antique shows for old bathroom accessories, vases, and platters. Give them new life as holders for soaps, toothbrushes, makeup bottles, and stacks of towels.

OLD TUB TIPS

IF YOU are a connoisseur of claw-foot tubs, such as the one *below*, follow these tips when shopping for a vintage model:

CONSIDER COSTS. Moderately clean tubs cost $100–$300 at the salvage yard. At specialty shops rarity determines the price; they usually run $800–$2,000. Reproduction hardware for an original model will cost $500–$800.

LOOK FOR FINE FINISHES. Because the new jacket on a reporcelainized tub is not as attractive or as long-lasting as the original coat, it's best to purchase a tub with the original enamel somewhat intact. Look into buying a claw-foot tub from someone who is ripping one out. The tub is more likely to be in better condition and have its legs and fixtures intact.

CHECK THE LEGS. It's a misconception that the legs on a claw-foot tub can be easily replaced. While there are millions of replacements available, finding a match may be impossible because there are no standard legs that fit. Make sure the tub you buy has four sturdy, matching legs.

COMPARE PLUMBING AND FIXTURES. Examine the hole arrangement for the faucet and drain. Typical faucet holes are set on a $3\frac{3}{8}$-inch center with the larger drain overflow centered between and beneath them. If the tub you're considering has any other hole arrangement, it must be fitted with its original valving because there is no way to replicate these variations.

REFRESHINGLY
SIMPLE

Give your bath a fresh new attitude with smooth surfaces, simple curves, and eye-catching color.

Sleek surfaces and stainless-steel and chrome accents give this bath *opposite* a modern and sophisticated look. Natural blond and red-dyed woods bring a feeling of warmth and coziness to the space.

IF YOU CONSIDER YOURSELF more new wave than old world, opt for a contemporary-style bath with clean lines, subtle contours, and lots of light as shown here. This pared-down look not only makes your bath easy to keep clean, but the soothing environment also helps ensure you'll start and end each day feeling relaxed and refreshed.

CONTEMPORARY CABINETS

For an uncluttered look, choose flat-fronted cabinets in a light, subtly grained wood, such as ash, birch, or maple, or with solid-color laminate fronts. For an up-to-date statement, choose cabinets in two different colors, a look that originated centuries ago when people outfitted rooms over decades rather than all at once. Here red-stained drawers advance from a granite-tile-topped double vanity. The color makes a bold statement, but it's

For more information on **contemporary style**, visit *HGTV.com/designstyles*

actually an aniline-dyed version of the naturally blond ash cabinets flanking the vanity base. For extra contemporary drama, sleek stainless-steel panels fill the spaces in front of the sinks typically covered with false drawers.

SLEEK SURFACES AND FIXTURES

Counters and floors should convey a similar streamlined look; tile, wood, and laminate make good choices. Here granite tiles visually connect counters, floors, and privacy partitions, keeping the focus on the colorful vanity. The shower and tub surround are also granite-wrapped: The curved tub platform sweeps into the adjacent shower to become a convenient bench seat. The elevated tub surround enables bathers to take advantage of the view through the picture window. For more information on choosing windows for your bath, turn the page.

Creamy white walls offer a clean backdrop for artwork and greenery. The wide curvaceous tub deck *above* provides display and storage space for candles and bathing supplies. The contoured shape repeats in the faucets and filler spouts.

CONTEMPORARY ELEMENTS

CLEAN LINES. Contemporary style is straightforward. Intricate details, such as ornate moldings and corbels, don't fit.

CURVES. Soften hard edges by tossing in a few curves, such as a rounded countertop or oval light fixtures.

WOODS. Select woods with uncomplicated grain patterns, such as maple, ash, birch, and walnut.

WINDOWS OF OPPORTUNITY

As the picture window on page 151 illustrates, welcome as much natural light into your bath as possible with well-placed windows, skylights, and glass doors.

WORKING GLASS Instead of opting for one larger, inoperable window above the tub, flank a fixed center window with two smaller working windows that can be used for ventilation *below*. If possible take advantage of the landscape for privacy. Plant tall pines or thick hedges, or install a tall fence.

OUTDOOR ACCESS Glass doors, such as the one *above*, bring in fresh air and sunlight, frame views, and provide a convenient spot for cleanup after gardening or yard work. Bath layouts that provide direct access to a pool, hot tub, or garden can also make your room feel like a luxurious retreat.

ATYPICAL SOLUTIONS If rooflines and fixture placement make windows difficult to place, think outside the box. In this attic bath *above* quarter-round windows installed above an existing sliding window soften the severe angles of the sloped roofline. The high placement of the windows alleviates the need for additional window dressings.

WINDOWS AND PRIVACY

WHEN ADDING windows and doors to your bath, make sure the amount of privacy you require is not compromised.

CHOOSE FROSTED OR STAINED GLASS to increase privacy without blocking out the light. Or use glass blocks as shown on page 32 to allow in light yet obscure the view. Some blocks distort views and conserve heat better than others, so choose a pattern that best matches your comfort level.

OPT FOR WINDOW TREATMENTS that cover windows and doors when needed but can be moved out of the way to allow in light and views when desired. Think of ease too. Motorized shades move up and down with the touch of a button. Or install blinds, shades, or shutters that cover the lower portion of the window for privacy and leave the upper panes bare for light.

WHEN COVERING YOUR WINDOWS with fabrics, avoid thick, heavy materials such as wool that may hold moisture and mildew. Instead choose quick-drying cottons and linens.

PROJECTS FOR YOUR BATH

Following are still more opportunities to put your plan for personal style into action. You'll find step-by-step instructions for recreating some of the projects shown in the preceding bathrooms as well as additional ideas for beautifying your bath. Each project is one you can do yourself to enliven your space with texture, color, pattern, and comfort. They are designed to help you give your bathroom a custom look for less. For pages 170–177 strap on your toolbelt and learn how easy it is to install wainscoting, tile flooring, crown molding, and a new faucet.

Drywall joint compound, randomly applied with a brush and later troweled, gives walls a handsome textural finish. The dark glaze settles into the recesses, fully enhancing the multi-dimensional treatment.

MATERIALS

Drywall joint compound

Semi-gloss latex paint, any color lighter than the glaze tint (pale taupe paint is used here)

Translucent water-base glaze (tinted to your preference with water-base stain or latex paint color)

TOOLS

Wide paintbrush(es)

Wallpaper paste brush (optional)

16-inch-long cement trowel

Container for mixing glaze

Stir stick

Clean rags

TEXTURE AND GLAZE WALLS

If you love the richly textured and glazed walls in the bathroom shown on pages 66–69, you can get the look at home following these step-by-step instructions. *Note: Clean the wall surface prior to following these instructions by removing wallpaper and/or dirt and debris.*

STEP BY STEP

1. Using a wide paintbrush or a wallpaper paste brush, apply drywall joint compound to the wall, working in one small 3×3-foot section at a time **(A)**. *Note: For a heavier, plasterlike texture, apply a thicker layer of compound but plan for an extended drying time.*

2. After applying compound to the section, immediately slap the side of the brush into the compound and pull it away, leaving peaks **(B)**. As the section dries, repeat Steps 1 and 2 on an adjacent section.

3. After the first section dries for 5 to 10 minutes (depending on the humidity level), gently smooth down the peaks by gliding lightly over the compound with the cement trowel **(C)**. Avoid leaving trowel-edge ridges. Repeat this troweling step after each subsequent section has dried for 5 to 10 minutes.

4. After finishing Step 3 on the entire wall, allow the compound to dry completely. *Note: The sheen of the compound will go from glossy to matte when it is dry. The length of drying time will vary depending on the humidity.*

5. Paint the wall with semi-gloss latex paint **(D)**; let dry completely.

6. Paint over the semi-gloss paint with a translucent water-base glaze. *Note: Darken the color glaze by adding water-base stain or latex paint color. The amount of tint you add depends on how prominent you want the recesses on the wall to appear. Apply the glaze with a brush (E), working in a small area at a time because water-base glaze dries quickly.*

7. Before the section of glaze dries, wipe away the glaze from the raised surfaces using a rag, allowing the darker glaze color to remain in the recesses to enhance the texture. Repeat the process to complete the wall; let dry.

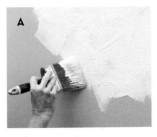

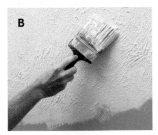

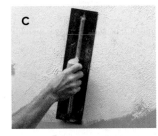

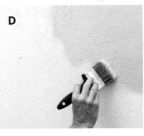

For more **projects and ideas** to spruce up your bath, visit *HGTV.com/bathrooms*

Turquoise-color tiles—inspired by the translucent glass sink—combine with tiles in blue, purple, and green to beautifully frame this mirror.

MATERIALS

1×2 pine lumber for frame (or select a lumber width ½ inch narrower than the tile to be used)

Wood glue

Small angle brackets and screws

Tile cement

Tile (in the desired size and color)

Grout

Mirror (see Step 6 for sizing)

Small nails or other hardware fasteners to hold mirror inside frame

Heavy-duty picture-hanging wire and nails (or two nails with large heads)

TOOLS

Circular saw

Miter box and backsaw or compound mitersaw

Carpenter's square

Cordless screwdriver

Half-moon blade or putty knife

Rags

Screwdriver and hammer

FRAME A
MIRROR WITH TILE

If your bathroom needs a boost on the style charts, surround a
purchased mirror with colorful tiles, as shown on pages 66–69.

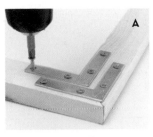

STEP BY STEP

1. Use a circular saw to cut four lengths of
   pine 1×2s for the frame—two pieces the
   combined length of the tiles to be used
   horizontally and two pieces the combined
   length of the tiles to be used vertically.
   (Account for the width of the grout lines
   as you calculate the finished size.)

2. Miter the ends of the wood frame pieces
   using a miter box and backsaw or a
   compound mitersaw.

3. Using a carpenter's square to check that the
   frame pieces are square, join each mitered
   corner with wood glue and angle brackets.
   Secure the brackets with screws **(A)**.

4. Spread tile cement over the frame using a
   half-moon blade **(B)** or a putty knife and
   lay the tiles **(C)**. The tiles should overlap
   the inside edge of the frame by at least ½
   inch to support the front surface of the
   mirror, which you will install in Step 6.

5. When the tiles are firmly set in the
   cement, grout the spaces between each
   tile, using your finger to smooth the grout
   (D). Wipe the tiles clean with a damp rag.
   Note: *A second buffing of the tiles is
   usually needed as the grout dries.*

6. Insert a mirror cut ⅛–¼ inch smaller than
   the inside dimensions of the frame; hold it
   in place with small nails or other hardware.
   Note: *Position the tip of a screwdriver on
   the nailhead* **(E)** *(or on other hardware
   fastener) and lightly tap the end of the
   screwdriver handle with a hammer to drive
   the fastener into place.*

7. Mount the mirror onto the wall by either
   hanging it with heavy-duty picture-hanging
   wire slipped over nails or by resting the
   inside of the top rail of the frame on two
   nails protruding from the wall by no more
   than ⅝ inch. In the latter case use nails
   with heads that will dig into the wood
   and prevent slippage.

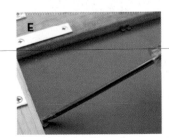

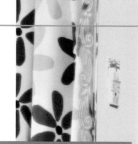

MATERIALS

Fabric for shower curtain
(45- or 54-inch wide)*

Fabric for bottom border
(contrasting or coordinating,
45- or 54-inch wide)*

Fabric for top band (to line
the back of the top edge of
the curtain)*

Fabric for tabs (coordinating
or contrasting)**

Matching thread

Paper for making a pattern

Rickrack (coordinating or
contrasting, any width)

Buttons

Plastic shower curtain liner

TOOLS

Cloth measuring tape

Scissors

Sewing machine

Pencil

Iron and ironing board

Straight pins

*See Step 1 for measurements.

**See Step 6 for measurements.

Multicolor floral fabric combines with
a colorful striped fabric to make this
curtain playful and fun. The tab-top
design of the curtain works with
casual and contemporary styles that
use a variety of fabric combinations.

TAB-TOP
SHOWER CURTAIN

Whether you want to make a color-happy shower curtain like the one shown in the bathroom on pages 104–107, or you envision another palette, use this technique to sew a stylish tab-top shower curtain using two or more coordinating fabrics.

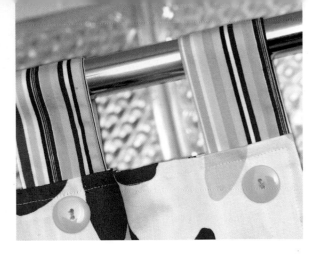

STEP BY STEP

1. For the main body of the curtain, cut two pieces of fabric measuring 65 inches long by the width of the fabric (fabric can be 45 or 54 inches wide). For the bottom border, cut two pieces of coordinating or contrasting fabric 19 ½ inches long by the fabric width. For the band of fabric that will line the back of the top edge of the curtain, cut one 4×74-inch strip of fabric.

2. Stack the two main pieces with right sides facing. Seam one long edge using a ½-inch seam allowance. Press the seam open. Re-cut the curtain to 80 inches wide.

3. Make a curving paper pattern or patterns to match the width of the curtain (with peaks and valleys as shallow or as deep as you wish). Use it as a cutting template by first pinning it in place along the top edge of the bottom border strip of fabric. Cut the curve following the pattern as a guide. Unpin the pattern and press under ½ inch of the curving edge of the fabric.

4. Lay the main curtain body face up and place the curving border section face up along the bottom edge of the main curtain body; topstitch the curving edge to the main curtain. Flip the main curtain over and trim away the excess fabric to follow the curve of the bottom border **(A)**. Flip the curtain back over so the right side faces up and zigzag-stitch rickrack along the curving seam.

5. Hem the long sides of the curtain: Fold 2 inches under and press. Fold another 2 inches under, press, and stitch.

6. Cut twelve 5×7-inch fabric strips for the tabs. Press under ⅜ inch on both long edges **(B)**. Fold in half lengthwise; press **(C)**.

7. Topstitch the long open edge of each tab. Fold the tab in half, top to bottom, and press. Align the cut edge of the tabs evenly across the top of the curtain. Baste the tabs in place.

8. Lay the 4-inch-wide top border strip on top of the tabs, with right sides of the border and the main curtain together and the tabs sandwiched between. Stitch with a ½-inch seam allowance **(D)**. Turn and press. Press under ½ inch of the lower edge of the strip. Topstitch the short ends and the long edge. Hand-stitch a button below each tab on the curtain.

9. Hem the lower edge of the curtain, following the same procedure for hemming in Step 5.

10. Thread the curtain onto a shower rod and pair with a plastic shower curtain liner.

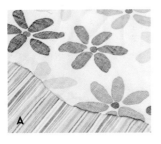

A

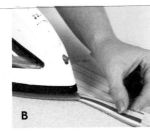

B

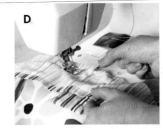

C

D

While this curtain takes on a hip image with a collage of office chairs from office supply catalogs, you could make a more romantic version with roses and flowers copied from a garden magazine or catalog.

MATERIALS

Plain purchased shower curtain (any color, cotton or 50/50 poly/cotton blend fabric)

Images from magazines, catalogs, calendars, or other copyright-free printed material

Iron-on transfer paper for ink-jet printers (optional if using a copy center)

TOOLS

Scissors

Scanner (or a color photocopier), computer, computer software that allows you to "flip" images or words, and a color ink-jet printer or access to a copy center capable of photocopying images onto iron-on transfer paper for ink-jet printers

Iron and a smooth, hard surface for ironing (such as a wooden easel top)

CHAIRS... CHAIRS... ch⟨s.... ch....

162

IRON-ON SHOWER CURTAIN

You won't have to search for just the right shower curtain when you purchase a plain curtain and create your own colorful pattern with this easy iron-on transfer process.

STEP BY STEP

1. Prewash the shower curtain.

2. Cut out the chosen images.

3. Scan the images into your computer and print onto transfer paper as directed by the manufacturer. Or color photocopy images onto transfer paper as directed by the manufacturer. You can also type words or phrases into a word processing program: "Flip" the wording (so it prints out mirror-reverse and will iron onto the curtain to read correctly) and then print the reversed words onto iron-on transfer paper (once again following the manufacturer's directions). **Note:** *If you are using a word-processing program and want to mirror-reverse, or "flip," the wording, look in the advanced options printing menus for a mirror-reverse option. You can also have the images (or words) color-copied onto transfer paper at a copy center. Remember you can reduce or enlarge the size of the images, if desired.*

4. Cut out transfer paper images along the perimeter **(A)**. If your fabric is a color other than white, cut away the white background areas around the image.

5. Place the cutout images facedown on the curtain panel, positioning the graphics to ensure you have a pleasing design and enough images. You can also experiment with border designs using repeating or random images. Once the images are in the desired positions, iron the back of the transfer paper following the manufacturer's directions **(B)**.

6. Remove the backing paper **(C)**.

7. When the curtain becomes soiled, wash it according to the shower curtain manufacturer's laundering directions, but avoid drying on high heat because the transferred images could melt.

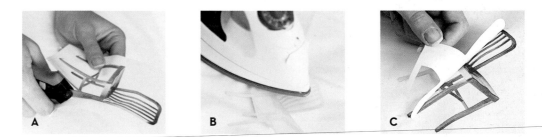

A   B   C

MATERIALS

Purchased bath mat

3 bath towels, coordinating
  or contrasting colors

Matching thread

Acrylic batting

Coordinating embroidery thread

TOOLS

Cloth measuring tape

Scissors

Straight pins

Sewing machine

Embroidery needle

SEW A BATH MAT

Introduce the softness and absorbency of terry cloth on the bathroom floor when you stitch this bath mat, shown in the bath on page 106, using colorful towels.

STEP BY STEP

1. Measure the length and width of a purchased bath mat. Divide the measurement of the long edge by 5. Add 2 inches to the measurements for the long edges and the short edges. Using these dimensions as a guide, cut five equal sections from three different colored bath towels.

2. Stack two of the color sections, pin together **(A)**, and stitch along one long edge, using a 1-inch seam allowance. Lay the two joined sections flat and lay another section on top, aligning the edges you plan to stitch. Pin together and stitch one long edge, using a 1-inch seam allowance. Continue the process until all five sections are stitched together. Press under 1 inch of the raw edges all the way around the terry cloth piece. Pin the joined terry cloth piece to the bath mat **(B)**.

3. Topstitch around three sides of the pinned pieces.

4. Insert a layer of batting cut to size. Topstitch the fourth edge closed.

5. Embroider flowers in the center of the middle three sections using a lazy daisy stitch **(C)**. Use the diagrams *right* as a guide. Wash the bath mat as you would towels.

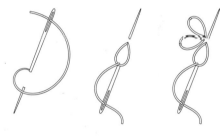

Lazy Daisy Stitch Diagrams

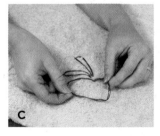

A layer of thick towels, batting, and a purchased bath mat make this customized bath mat *opposite* cushiony and comfortable underfoot.

MATERIALS

2 coordinating fabrics*

Paper for making a pattern

Matching thread

Coordinating rickrack (any width)

Hook-and-loop tape

TOOLS

Cloth measuring tape

Pencil

Scissors

Straight pins

Iron and ironing board

Sewing machine

*See Steps 1–3 for cutting instructions.

Soften the appearance of a pedestal or wall-hung sink with a skirt that hangs to the floor. Lift the skirt *opposite above* to discover hidden storage space.

SNAZZY SINK SKIRT

Bring color and style to a wall-hung or pedestal sink, such as the one shown on pages 104–105, by fashioning your own fabric sink skirt.

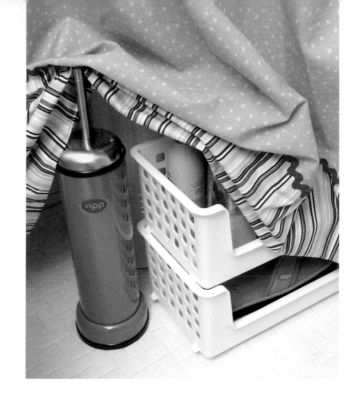

STEP BY STEP

1. Measure the front edge of the sink from wall to wall. Multiply the measurement by 1½ for the skirt fullness. Add another 4 inches for the side hems.

2. Measure the length of the skirt from the top edge of the sink to the floor. Add 4 inches for the hems.

3. To size the top portion of the skirt, use three-quarters of the length measurement; one-quarter of the length measurement to determine the border fabric dimensions.

4. Make a curving paper pattern (or patterns) to extend across the width of the skirt and

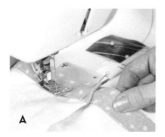

A

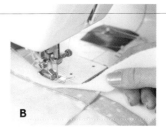

B

use it as a cutting template by pinning it in place along the top edge of the bottom border strip of fabric. Cut the curve following the pattern as a guide. Unpin the pattern and press under ½ inch of the curving edge of the fabric.

5. Lay the main skirt body face up and place the curving border section face up along the bottom edge of the skirt body; topstitch the curving edge to the main skirt. Flip the main skirt over and trim away the excess fabric on the main skirt to follow the curve of the bottom border. Flip the skirt back over so the right side faces up and zigzag-stitch rickrack along the curving seam.

6. Hem the top and bottom edges of the

skirt: Fold 1 inch under and press. Fold another 1 inch under, press, and stitch. Follow the same procedure to hem each long side of the skirt.

7. Find the center of the skirt along the top edge and mark with a straight pin. Pin along the top edge, spacing evenly to match the finished sink measurement. Baste the pleats in place (A).

8. Stitch hook-and-loop tape on the top edge of the back of the skirt, using two rows of stitches (B).

9. Apply the adhesive-back half of the hook-and-loop tape along the front top edge of the sink. Hang the sink skirt on the sink, joining the two halves of the hook-and-loop tape.

MATERIALS

Drop cloths

Low-tack painter's tape

Drywall surfacing compound

Latex primer (tinted to match base coat)

Latex paint, cream or other light color for the base coat

Purchased stencil, old-world-style design or other motif

Spray stencil adhesive (optional)

Artist's oil paint in raw umber, earthy green, and burnt sienna*

Oil-base glaze (tinted 90 percent gray, 10 percent purple)

TOOLS

Putty knife

Fine-grit sandpaper

Lint-free rag

Stir stick

Paint roller and tray

Paintbrush

Stencil brushes (3)

Cheesecloth

Plastic scrubbing sponge (optional)

* This paint is available in ½-ounce tubes at art supply stores.

STENCIL ON OLD-WORLD STYLE

This unusual stencil treatment *opposite* looks as though it has been there for years. Invest a few days in this beautiful "aged" technique and enjoy the look for years. Practice on poster board, following the photos *right,* before executing the technique on your walls. To reduce the chance of smudging, it is recommended that you complete one wall at a time; you may prime and base-coat the walls in one work session, but perform Steps 4–5 after the adjoining wall(s) is completely dry.

STEP BY STEP

1. Protect floors, fixtures, and furniture with drop cloths; protect moldings with low-tack painter's tape. Patch any holes in the walls with drywall surfacing compound and a putty knife; let dry. Sand smooth, then wipe with a lint-free rag.

2. With a large roller, apply primer to the walls; let dry.

3. Apply the base color **(A)** to the walls; let dry.

4. Secure the stencil to the wall in the desired location with low-tack painter's tape or use spray stencil adhesive. Using artist's oil paints and a different stencil brush for each of the three colors, dab a small amount of each oil paint on the open portions of the stencil. Dab randomly and in a circular motion **(B)** until you achieve the desired intensity, blending the colors for a subtle look. Remove the stencil, wipe its back with a lint-free rag to remove paint smudges, and repeat the process, placing the next stencil far enough away so there's no overlap. Continue until you've completed the wall; let dry 24 hours.

5. Pour oil-base glaze into a paint tray. Apply a light coat of the glaze over the stencil pattern **(C)**. To give the appearance of more age, let the glaze dry, then apply a second coat. While the glaze is still tacky, pat down the wall with cheesecloth to remove brush marks; let dry 24 hours. If desired very lightly "sand" random areas with a plastic scrubbing sponge to soften the design.

A detailed stencil design, applied with tinted glaze, lends an air of sophistication to a small bathroom *opposite*. Three colors of paint (layered over a stencil) create the aged look.

INSTALL BEADED-BOARD WAINSCOTING

Dress up the walls in your bathroom in vintage style by adding beaded-board wainscoting.

MATERIALS

Beaded-board panels

Thin blocks of wood (for stacking panels during acclimation)

Primer and satin-finish paint in the desired color

Construction adhesive

Finishing nails and brads

Cap molding (enough to finish top edges of installed panels)

Base molding (enough to finish bottom edges of installed panels)

Electrical outlet box extenders

Wood filler or paintable putty

Paintable caulk

TOOLS

Measuring tape

Water level

Pencil

Chalk line

Jigsaw or keyhole saw

Handsaw or circular saw

Stir stick

Paintbrush or roller and tray

Safety goggles

Hammer and nail set or pneumatic nail gun

Miter box and backsaw

Caulk gun

Fine-grit sandpaper

Tack cloth

Panels that simulate beaded board lend a charming cottage or vintage feel to a bathroom and are easier to install than individual tongue-and-groove planks. Some panels are available in white. Other panel types can be stained or painted white or another color.

STEP BY STEP

Note: *Although some beaded-board panel products arrive cut to wainscot height, full-size panels can be cost-effective. (Do the math: 96 inches divided by three equals 32 inches, so you could get three 32×48-inch pieces of wainscoting out of one standard 4×8-foot panel.)* **Also** *follow the manufacturer's recommendations when installing any product and use proper safety equipment. The information presented here gives you a general overview of wainscoting installation, but the manufacturer may have special instructions for its own materials.* **Finally** *wear safety goggles whenever you operate power equipment, such as a power saw or pneumatic nail gun.*

1. Determine the desired wainscoting height (see "Wainscoting Height" *opposite* for recommended heights).

2. Bring the panels into your house for a couple of days before starting your project to let them acclimate to the house, limiting expansion or contraction after installation. Stack the panels horizontally, with thin blocks of wood between each sheet to allow air to circulate.

3. Most floors are not level. Installing the wainscoting from a level line on the wall will help hide imperfections. At one point on the wall, measure the desired height of your wainscoting (remember that cap molding above the panels will add slightly to the finished height). From that point use the water level to draw a horizontal line with a pencil **(A)** then extend it around the room. **Note:** *It's much easier to extend a level line around a room with a water level*

than with a traditional carpenter's level. Water levels, which are available at home centers, use long tubes filled with water. They make it easy to mark points throughout the room at exactly the same height. Use a chalk line to connect the points **(B)**. **Note:** *The line you marked around the room is the top of the panel installation. The base molding installed in Step 7 will cover the bottom edge of the beaded-board paneling.*

4. Cut the panels to height. Measure the positions of outlets or light switches on the wall; transfer those measurements to the back of each panel. Use a jigsaw or keyhole saw to cut the holes **(C)**.

5. If the panels aren't pre-painted or aren't the desired color, paint them before installation. Roll on a coat of primer; let dry. Roll on two coats of paint; let the first coat dry before applying the second.

6. Squeeze a zigzag bead of construction adhesive onto the wall side of the panel **(D)**. Attach the panels to the wall, spacing nails along the edges of the panel as indicated by the manufacturer. If you hammer the nails by hand, use a nail set **(E)** to indent the nail so it can be covered with paintable putty. Space and overlap panels according to the manufacturer's recommendations; this allows for expansion and contraction caused by temperature and humidity changes.

7. Use brads to nail cap molding at the top of the wainscoting panels. Use a miter box and backsaw **(F)** to cut the angled joints where walls meet. Install new base molding or reinstall the existing molding **(G)** with brads. After installing the panels, install a box extender at each electrical point to contain the wires.

8. Fill any visible nail holes with putty **(H)** and caulk any gaps as necessary. Lightly sand filled holes and wipe with a tack cloth. Touch up filled spots with paint if needed.

MATERIALS

Cement board

1½-inch galvanized roofing
  nails or 1¼-inch cement
  board screws

Ceramic tiles

Tile adhesive

Tile spacers
  (in the desired width)

Grout
  (in the desired color)

Grout sealer

TOOLS

Tools to remove old
  flooring (optional)

Hammer or power
  screwdriver

Measuring tape

Straightedge

Pencil

Utility knife

Chalk line

Notched trowel

Needle-nose pliers

Grout float

Bucket and sponge

Soft, clean rags

White vinegar (optional)

Small stiff-bristle brush

TILE A BATHROOM FLOOR

Does your floor need a facelift? Don't
call in the professionals—keep money in
your pocket by tackling the job yourself!

STEP BY STEP

1. If needed remove old flooring down to
    the subfloor. Use a hammer or screwdriver
    and roofing nails or cement board screws
    to attach cement board to the subfloor
    as a water-resistant underlayment.
    Note: *To cut cement board, place the
    printed side up and measure and mark
    the cutting line with a straightedge and
    pencil. Use the straightedge and a utility
    knife to score the cutting line and snap
    the board along the line. Flip the board
    over to make a second pass with the
    utility knife for a clean cut.*

New ceramic tile for the floor
and tub surround *left* provides
a refreshing starting point for
this bathroom makeover.

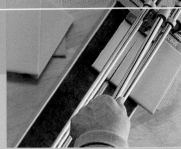

CUTTING TILES

FOLLOW THESE INSTRUCTIONS to cut tiles. Remember to wear safety goggles and work gloves.

LAY THE TILE FACE UP, directly on top of the whole tile it will adjoin. Butt another whole tile against the edge you're cutting to and overlap the tile to be cut. Scribe the face of the first tile along the edge of the lapped one, etching through the glaze; this helps minimize chipping when you cut the tile.

FOR STRAIGHT CUTS, lay the tile face up on the bed of a snap-cutting tool *above*. Position your score mark under the scoring wheel of the tool and lock the tile into place with the adjustable brace. Apply firm steady pressure as you draw the scoring wheel across the tile. After scoring park the wheel in the slot above the tile and exert firm downward pressure on the lever arm. The tile should snap apart neatly along the scored line. A few tiles will break no matter how careful you are, so expect to redo some cuts.

FOR IRREGULAR CUTS, use either a rod saw or a pair of tile nippers. Before using either tool, practice on a piece of scrap tile to get a feel for the technique then proceed cautiously.

2. Measure the width of the floor, halve that number, and pencil a line at that point across the floor (or snap a chalk line). Repeat the process to find the halfway point for the length of the room and pencil a mark across the floor from wall to wall. (You'll end up with two lines that intersect at the center of the room.)

3. Before applying tile adhesive, place the corner of the first tile at the point where the penciled lines intersect, and center other tiles along one line, leaving about ¼ inch between them for grout lines. Arrange the tiles to minimize cutting. Mark their location with a pencil, then remove them. Apply tile adhesive to a 3-foot section of the floor using a notched trowel **(A)**.

4. Following the pencil marks, lay the first tile in the adhesive. Use tile spacers for even grout lines **(B)**.

5. Continue laying tile until you get to the walls; cut remaining tiles with a scorer to fit (see "Cutting Tiles" *top right*). Let adhesive dry as recommended by the manufacturer.

6. Remove the spacers with needle-nose pliers, then apply grout with a float **(C)**. Let the grout set about 15 minutes or for the time recommended by the manufacturer. With a damp sponge, wipe the grout residue from the faces of the tiles **(D)**. Rinse the sponge in a pail of water after each pass. After rinsing, let dry, then remove the final haze with a soft, clean rag or scrub it off with water or a solution of water and white vinegar. Dump the rinse water outdoors; grout deposits can clog waste lines.

7. Let the grout dry as recommended by the manufacturer. As soon as it has dried thoroughly (usually about three days), apply one or two coats of grout sealer with a small stiff-bristle brush. Use a soft, dry cloth to remove excess sealer from the tile as you work; some sealers can discolor tile finishes.

Boxy bathrooms gain architectural interest when you add crown molding where the walls meet the ceiling.

MATERIALS

Crown molding

Satin-finish or semi-gloss latex paint (in the desired color) or stain (in the desired color) and clear sealer

Extra blocks for practice cuts of similar pieces

Finishing nails

Caulk, wood filler, or patching compound

TOOLS

Paintbrushes

Stir stick

Stud finder

Pencil

Miter box and backsaw

Coping saw with spare blades

Measuring tape

Small flat and round files

Fine-grit sandpaper

Hammer and nail set or pneumatic finish nailer*

Drill

Caulking gun (for painted moldings only)

Putty knife

*This tool is very helpful in place of the hammer and nail set listed above; pneumatic finish nailers are available for rent.

INSTALL CROWN MOLDING

You don't have to move walls to create a new look for your bathroom. Adding crown molding instills your space with style and definition, bridging the junction between walls and ceiling, a prominent location where the architectural accent can shine.

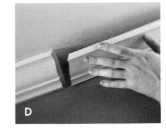
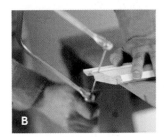

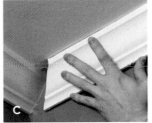

STEP BY STEP

1. Paint or seal, stain, and varnish the molding before installing; let dry.

2. Moldings should be nailed to studs or ceiling joists rather than directly to the drywall. Scan the walls and ceiling with a stud finder; make light pencil marks to indicate the studs and joists. Mark a few inches away from the wall-ceiling joint so you can still see your marks after you put the molding in place. ***Note:*** *Work from one point around the perimeter of the room. That way you'll have only one "closer" piece that must fit precisely against adjacent moldings on each end.*

3. When two molding pieces meet at an outside corner, use miter cuts (cutting the pieces at 45-degree angles with a miter box and backsaw) at the meeting end of each. When moldings meet at an inside corner, irregular wall surfaces usually create a poor fit if you use mitered ends. Instead cut one molding with a square end and the other with an inside 45-degree miter **(A)**; then use a coping saw to cut along the contoured edge of the mitered molding, removing the exposed end-grain stock **(B)**. File and sand the cut until the contour fits snugly against the adjacent molding **(C)**. Use extra blocks of molding to practice and make repeated test fits and trim cuts until you get it right.

4. Nail each piece in place, but don't countersink the nails yet. If you're power-nailing with a pneumatic nailing gun, drive in only enough nails to hold the molding securely; that way you can remove molding with little or no damage to the pieces if needed. ***Note:*** *If you're using a wide crown molding, install a hidden nailer strip behind it to provide more surface area to nail into.*

5. When a long wall forces you to create a joint between two pieces of molding, cut a scarf joint (overlapping 45-degree beveled ends) for a less conspicuous joint. The exception for this is wide crown molding. Making angled cuts in this width of molding is difficult, so pieces probably will fit better with square cuts butted against each other creating a butt joint. If possible always start by precision-cutting one end of the molding and leaving the other end about ¼ inch too long, then position it in place to mark the precise length to cut **(D)**.

6. After properly fitting the molding pieces, finish driving and countersinking the nails **(E)**. For nails near ends, drill pilot holes to prevent splitting the wood. Fill nail holes with wood filler or patching compound, then sand. Use caulk or wood filler for small gaps at corners **(F)**. Conceal nail holes using a putty knife and patching compound or wood filler and paint or stain to touch up.

A new, classic two-handle faucet complements the custom-made concrete countertop on this vanity shown on page 93.

MATERIALS

Mineral spirits or denatured alcohol

Rubber gasket or length of rope caulk

Plumber's putty

Supply tubes (optional)

New faucet

New pop-up drain (usually comes with the faucet)

TOOLS

Adjustable wrench

Screwdriver

Putty knife

Plastic scrubber or single-edge razor blade

Basin wrench

Groove-joint pliers

INSTALL A BATHROOM FAUCET

Update your bathroom with a new faucet for the sink. Follow these instructions to install it yourself and save the cost of labor.

STEP BY STEP

Note: There are variations, but most bathroom sinks have three holes on the deck ledge to accommodate either double-handle or single-handle faucets. If the distance between the centers of the outside holes measures 8 inches, the sink is designed for a faucet with separate handles and spout. More common is 4-inch center-to-center spacing, for faucets with the spout and handles integrated into a single base. Installation is similar to a kitchen faucet, but bathroom faucets require a pop-up stopper assembly.

1. Shut off water at the stop valves. From below, use a wrench to disconnect the supply tubes and the mounting nuts from the old faucet stems. Loosen the screw that holds the clevis strap to the lift rod, pinch the spring clip **(A)**, and slide the clevis strap off the pivot rod.

2. Pull out the old faucet and clean the sink deck, removing the old putty with a putty knife. Clean the surface with a plastic scrubber and mineral spirits or denatured alcohol, or a single-edge razor blade. Fit a rubber gasket (or a length of rope caulk or putty) onto the base of the new faucet, and set in place **(B)**.

3. Have a helper hold the faucet straight while you tighten the mounting nuts from below. After hand-tightening use a basin wrench to tighten mounting nuts **(C)**. Connect the supply tubes to the faucet, tightening with an adjustable wrench.

4. You can use the existing drain body, but the new faucet should come with one. Follow the manufacturer's instructions to install the drain body and the pop-up drain. With the stopper closed all the way, slide the clevis strap onto the lift rod and the pivot rod, using the spring clip to hold it in place. Tighten the setscrew that holds the strap to the lift rod. Reconnect the trap **(D)** with the groove-joint pliers.

5. Make sure the stopper seals tightly when the lift rod is pulled up and it opens fully when the rod is pushed down. To adjust, loosen the setscrew **(E)** and move the clevis strap up or down. Open the stop valves, then remove the faucet aerator and test the water flow.

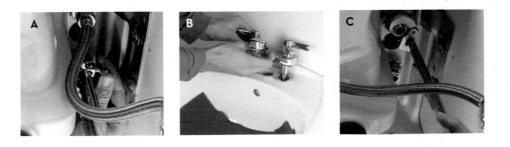

PLANNING GUIDE AND **ARRANGING** KIT

After taking in all these functional and stylish bathrooms and the elements that make them happen, you likely have dozens of terrific ideas. Now you're ready to take an exciting step and align those needs and wants into a cohesive and workable plan. In this section you'll analyze the bathroom you have now to determine what works and what doesn't and also to anticipate future needs. Budgeting begins here too, with a cost chart to help you establish realistic goals. Then work with the bath arranging kit to find the floor plan that's right for you.

A LITTLE HOMEWORK

Whether your bath is in need of a decorative facelift or a major overhaul, these tips can help you invest your dollars wisely.

Before you begin your bath makeover, analyze your present bath, listing what you like and dislike about it. (The quiz *opposite* can aid you in this step.) This will help you determine if your renovation will be cosmetic, structural, or both. Changing flooring, cabinets, and countertops may transform a dreary decor, but adding storage and counter space or reworking traffic flow generally requires more costly remodeling.

FUTURE PLANS Assess your personal situation including how you will be using your bath now and in the coming years. If you plan to be living in your house for 10 or more years, greater remodeling expenses are justified than if you will be moving within a few years. Although an updated bath makes a good selling point, keep the overall value of your home in mind if you want to recoup renovation costs within a short period.

NITTY-GRITTY DETAILS Before making any purchases take accurate measurements of your bath and then visit model displays to determine the features and components you want. If you will be expanding your space consider how much more room you will need for the amenities you desire. As you shop

different retailers ask for price quotes. Be certain that the dollar amount each retailer supplies is for the comparable size and quality of fixtures and cabinets. Clarify delivery and installation changes, warranties, and service options. (You can also estimate costs of common components using the chart on pages 182–183.) Whether your budget is large or small, make quality a priority. Leaky faucets, sagging doors, and sticking drawers are irritating and may be difficult, if not impossible, to repair.

THE BOTTOM LINE Getting price quotes for all the products you want accounts for the "hard costs" of your bath makeover, but these numbers don't tell the complete story. These costs may equal less than half a project's total cost once you add in labor and unseen material costs such as flooring underlayments, plumbing updates, and additional electrical lines.

Just how much of your budget goes to labor depends on the scope of the project and the region where you live. In a simple tear-out-and-replace job in the Heartland, labor may be only one-third of the total costs. On the coasts labor costs may double that amount. If there are major structural changes such as moving and removing walls, windows, and doors, the percentage will also be greater.

Plus certain kinds of cabinets, surfaces, and fixtures are more difficult to install than others which affects labor costs. Be sure to ask questions before settling on any particular component: A look-alike may be more cost effective.

Most bath designers agree that cabinetry and fixture costs are the biggest variables in a bath budget and the easiest place to save or splurge. The key to gauging cabinetry costs is counting "boxes." A box is an individual cabinet unit, such as a base cabinet, a wall cabinet, or a set of drawers. Per box averages (often listed in manufacturer literature as the average cost of a 24-inch base cabinet) may cost anywhere from $200 for stock cabinets to $2,000 for custom cabinets. The more boxes you use, the higher the cabinetry cost. Imported fixtures typically cost more than domestic fixtures, so shop several places and choose wisely.

If, after adding up all the variables, a totally new bath seems too costly, make only cosmetic changes now (as with the bathrooms featured on pages 92 and 110) and wait a few years before undertaking a major renovation. As technology advances and styles evolve, requirements for that "perfect bath" will continue to keep you wanting for more.

PRIORITY CHECKLIST

**Planning the bathroom you want requires that you understand the one you have.
Then you need to think about what you'd like to change and how you'd change it.**

This quiz will help you identify what kind of bathroom you're living with now, what its advantages and drawbacks are, what your needs are, and what you'd like to have in your new bathroom.

First evaluate the bathroom you have now using this list of questions *right*. Use the box beside each question to indicate how important it is to rectify any problems you identify. Use the following number system or devise your own: 1 = high priority, 2 = medium priority, 3 = low priority.

Consider how higher-priority problems may be solved by a renovation or avoided if you're building a new bathroom.

With your prioritized bath uses in mind, also note which fixtures (both a bathtub and a shower, for example), storage needs, and special amenities (such as a towel warmer) your new or remodeled bathroom will have.

Refer to this questionnaire as you continue to plan your bathroom. Take it with you when you talk to your bathroom designer, architect, or contractor.

For more information on **designing your own bath,** visit *HGTV.com/bathplanner*

BATH QUIZ

Use this list of questions to identify the features of your current bath that you want to change when you build or remodel. Use each box to note the priority:
1 = high priority, 2 = medium priority, 3 = low priority.

STORAGE
- [ ] Are bathing linens within reach of bathing facilities?
- [ ] Is there a place for soiled laundry (chute, hamper, other)?
- [ ] Is there enough storage for linens and cleaning supplies?

BATHING
- [ ] Are bathing facilities suitable for the intended use?
- [ ] Is the hot water supply adequate for the bathers' use?
- [ ] Is water quality adequate, or does it require softening?
- [ ] Are bathing areas adequately lit?
- [ ] Are bathing areas easily accessible to everyone?
- [ ] Do floors, tubs, and shower stalls feature nonslip flooring?

PRIVACY
- [ ] Are windows and treatments placed to allow both light and privacy?
- [ ] Are the toilet and bathing areas secluded from vanity areas?
- [ ] Are latches and locks secure and easy for all users to operate?

SURFACES
- [ ] Are you pleased with the current surfaces?
- [ ] Are the surfaces easy to clean?
- [ ] Do they tolerate standing water and high humidity?

LIGHT AND VIEWS
- [ ] Is your bathroom shadowy?
- [ ] Do you have enough window light?

TRAFFIC
- [ ] Do entries block fixtures or storage when open?
- [ ] Are paths from the toilet to bathing areas to grooming areas logical?

AMENITIES
Would you like any of these special features?
- [ ] Soaking tub
- [ ] Whirlpool tub
- [ ] Two-person shower
- [ ] Steam shower
- [ ] Luxury fixed showerheads
- [ ] Handheld showerhead
- [ ] Shower with body sprays
- [ ] Dual vanities
- [ ] Full-length mirror
- [ ] Bidet
- [ ] Towel warmer
- [ ] Radiant heat flooring
- [ ] Sauna

BATH COMPONENT COSTS Start calculating your bath costs with our product listing. Except where noted, prices do not include labor and installation.

ITEM	DESCRIPTION	COST
CABINETRY	READY-MADE offers limited choices in sizes, woods, finishes, and door styles; quality ranges depending on cabinetry line	$100–$200 per linear foot w/o hardware
	SEMICUSTOM offers a wide range of sizes, woods, finishes, and door styles; good quality	$125–$650 per linear foot w/o hardware
	CUSTOM offers any size, shape, and finish; exotic woods available; high attention to detail	$500–$1,000 per linear foot w/o hardware
COUNTERTOPS	CERAMIC TILE basic, glass, or art tile significantly higher; priced per sq. ft.	$2–$10
	WOOD installed, per sq. ft.	$20–$80
	LAMINATE installed, per linear ft.	$30–$40
	QUARTZ installed, per sq. ft.	$35–$115
	SOLID-SURFACING installed, per sq. ft.	$45–$85
	STONE OR CONCRETE installed, per sq. ft.	$60–$100+
SINK FAUCETS	BASIC chrome or colored epoxy, single lever or close-set two handle	$60–$100
	SOLID BRASS construction, widespread, some fancier looks and finishes	$125–$200
	WIDESPREAD OR WALL-MOUNT high-quality finish, designer looks	$250–$600
	UNUSUAL HIGH-STYLE DESIGN OR IMPORT	$600–$1,200
SHOWERHEADS/ TUB SPOUTS	BASIC FIXED SHOWERHEAD and tub spout; pressure-balance/anti-scald features available	$75–$150
	ADJUSTABLE-HEIGHT handheld shower with metal hose	$100–$700
	WIDESPREAD tub filler spout with separate handles	$250–$1,000
	JETTED SHOWER SYSTEM body sprays with fixed and/or handheld showerhead	$300–$5,000
	HIGH-STYLE or three-handle fixed showerhead, better-quality valves	$350–$1,200
FLOORING	VINYL SHEET	$6–$39 per sq. yd.
	VINYL TILE	$1–$6 per sq. ft.
	CERAMIC TILE art tile significantly higher	$2–$7 per tile
	LINOLEUM	$3–$6 per sq. ft.
	CORK	$4–$11 per sq. ft.
	LAMINATE priciest: tile look	$4–$13 per sq. ft.
	SLATE, GRANITE, OR LIMESTONE	$5–$30 per sq. ft.
	MARBLE OR TRAVERTINE	$5–$30 per sq. ft.
	HARDWOOD solid or engineered	$8–$30 per sq. ft.

ITEM	DESCRIPTION	COST
BIDET	STANDARD COLOR/STYLE vertical or horizontal spray	$350–$500
	HIGH-END color or design	$500–$1,300
	CLEANSING SEAT heated, air dryer	$700–$1,400
TOILET	BASIC gravity-fed (siphon-action) two-piece, white	$100–$200
	ONE-PIECE OR STYLISH TWO-PIECE white or color, pressure-assisted or gravity-fed	$250–$700
	DESIGNER ONE-PIECE, special hardware or color (priciest: hand-painted)	$900–$1,600+
SHOWER ENCLOSURE	BASIC PLASTIC OR FIBERGLASS MODULE 32×32-inch to 48×32-inch, walls and base	$170–$450
	CORNER SHOWER with glass door, chrome or brass trim	$450–$1,900
	ALCOVE SHOWER with base, solid-surfacing walls, glass door	$1,500–$4,600
	CURVED CORNER SHOWER base and zero-clearance sliding door	$1,800+
SINK	BASIC WHITE CHINA drop-in, undermount, or pedestal; add $50–$100 for color	$100–$200
	PEDESTAL OR DROP-IN sink with greater detailing or period style	$225–$600+
	SOLID-SURFACING VANITY TOP with single integral sink, basic colors	$300–$1,000
	VESSEL above-counter bowl	$300–$2,000
	CONSOLE priciest: handcrafted furniture base	$600–$3,000+
	HAND-PAINTED high-end import	$750–$3,000+
SOAKING TUB	BASIC 5-foot enameled steel or fiberglass tub	$90–$175
	CAST IRON	$250–$1,300
	ACRYLIC	$300–$1,000
	FREESTANDING tub (claw-foot, slipper-style, pedestal)	$1,600–$3,700
WHIRLPOOL TUB	BASIC 5-foot model, 1–1.5 horsepower motor	$600–$1,500
	LARGE, LUXURIOUS models with 4 to 10 jets, 2–3 horsepower variable-speed motor, heater	$2,000–$4,500
	UNUSUAL WATER ELEMENTS shiatsu, waterfall	$5,000–$7,000+

CHOOSE THE PROS AND SURVIVE THE MESS

Whether you're searching for an architect, an interior designer, or a remodeling contractor, you can use these tactics to track down the best professionals to design and execute your bath decorating or remodeling project. Then follow the survival tips to make the best of the mess.

GATHER

Collect the names of professionals to investigate and interview. Ask friends and colleagues for suggestions and recommendations. Identify local referrals with the help of professional organizations, such as the American Institute of Architects (AIA), 800/242-3837, website: aia.org; the National Association of Home Builders Remodelers Council (NAHB), 800/368-5242 ext. 8216, website: nahb.com; the National Association of the Remodeling Industry (NARI), 800/611-6274, website: nari.org; or the American Society of Interior Designers (ASID), 202/546-3480, website: asid.org. These websites can help you find a contractor in your area: handymanonline.com; improvenet.com; remodelnet.com; and homeownersreferral.com.

EXPLORE

Call the professionals on your list—you should have four or five from each profession—and ask for references. Contact the clients they name and ask them to recount their positive and negative experiences. Also, if you've seen a recent decorating or remodeling project that you like, contact the homeowners and ask about their experience and results.

EVALUATE

Based on these references, interview your top three choices and tour some of their finished projects. Savvy architects and contractors will ask you questions as well to determine your expectations and needs. You should come away from each interview and tour with an idea of the quality of their work and how well your personalities and visions for the project match.

SOLICIT

To narrow your choices, it may be worth the additional cost to solicit preliminary drawings from each professional. This is a great way to test your working relationship and to gather options. Also ask contractors for bids. Don't base your decision on cost alone, but weigh what you learned in the interview with the thoroughness of the bid itself.

SIGN UP

Before beginning a project with any professional, have the facts on paper to protect you legally before, during, and after the work is done. Define the scope of the project and fees as specifically as possible. The contract should include a clear description of the work to be done, materials that will be required, and who will supply them. It should also spell out commencement and completion dates, any provisions relating to timeliness, and your total costs (subject to additions and deductions by a written change order only). Payments should be tied to work stages; be wary of any contractor who wants a lot of money up front. If ordering certain materials and fixtures needs to be done weeks in advance (to allow time for manufacturing or overseas delivery), get a list of all those items and their cost before committing to up-front money. If possible make out these initial checks to the subcontractors and retailers directly.

SURVIVAL TIPS

When your bath transforms into a construction zone, the mess can make you wonder if your life will ever be back to normal. To ensure the minor inconveniences of a bath makeover or a remodeling project don't become major headaches, discuss cleanup with your contractor before work begins. Have a team meeting with all the key professionals and ask for an overview of the entire project so together you can develop a plan to minimize disruption. Ask workers to arrive and leave at reasonable hours. **Noise is inevitable.** Understand that if you set shorter workdays, you will also be setting, and possibly lengthening, the duration of the project. Let the contractor know in advance if there are any times, such as holidays or special family events, when your house will be off-limits. **Set up "temporary rooms."** If you're remodeling more than one bath, ask for a timeline that keeps one of the baths in service until the next one is ready to use again. If you don't want workers to use your restrooms, set up a portable toilet near the entrance to the remodeling area. **Be flexible.** No matter how meticulously you schedule your project, there is bound to be a surprise or two. Go with the flow and be willing to change out a discontinued fabric, tile, or fixture.

BATH ARRANGING KIT

**Here is everything you need—templates of common bath components and grid paper—
to allow you to experiment with floor plan arrangements for your new bathroom.**

Even if you plan to work with a professional designer, you'll find it beneficial to "test drive" some potential layout ideas for your bathroom. Share these preliminary plans with your designer to best communicate your needs and the floor-plan arrangements that make you feel most comfortable.

Photocopy the grid paper on page 187 and plot out the dimensions of your planned bathroom space. If you're remodeling within an existing bathroom space, take careful measurements, including the locations of doors and windows, and transfer those to the grid paper. (1 square equals 1 square foot of floor space.) Use the architectural symbols *below* to mark the position of existing architectural features. If you plan to add some of these features, use a different color to indicate what is new, such as built-ins or new fixtures. Use dotted lines to mark obstructions, including prominent light fixtures and angled

ceilings. If you're building a new addition, mark the existing structure in one color and use a different color to mark the addition. Whether your bathroom will be remodeled, part of an addition, or located in a new house, plot the space as well as its relationship to adjacent areas, including any closet, dressing room, hall, bedroom, and sitting or snacking areas.

Then photocopy and cut out the templates *below*, *right*, and *on page 186* and arrange and rearrange the components on your grid paper plan. If you own an existing piece of furniture that you want to include in your bathroom plan, such as an ottoman or dressing table, measure the piece, draw it to scale (1 square on the grid paper equals 1 square foot of space), and cut out the new template to use on the grid plan. Once you find one or two arrangements that you like best, trace the templates directly onto the grid paper.

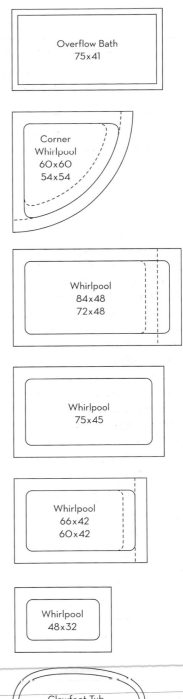

Overflow Bath
75x41

Corner
Whirlpool
60x60
54x54

Whirlpool
84x48
72x48

Whirlpool
75x45

Whirlpool
66x42
60x42

Whirlpool
48x32

Clawfoot Tub
66x36

Note: Tub depths vary
depending on manufacturer

$ LIGHT OR OTHER SWITCH

⊕   LIGHT FIXTURE (Not Lamp)

S   S₃   ⊕

SINGLE-POLE   3-WAY   DUPLEX
SWITCH   SWITCH   OUTLET

TV   20A   ⊙

TV ANTENNA   AIR-   FLOOR
OUTLET   CONDITIONING   OUTLET
        (20 amp) OUTLET

▲   F   ⊔

TELEPHONE   CEILING FAN   BELL

DOUBLE-HUNG SASH

CASEMENT SASH OPENING IN OR OUT

DOOR SWINGING IN OR OUT

BIFOLD DOORS

SLIDING DOORS – 6 or 8 ft.

CASED OPENING (Passage)

FIREPLACE (with Mantel)

INCANDESCENT LIGHT OUTLETS

○   ⊗

RECESSED   WALL
CEILING   BRACKET

⊕   ⊣○⊢

CEILING   TRACK LIGHTING

STAIR

RADIATOR

DOUBLE DOOR

COVERED RADIATOR

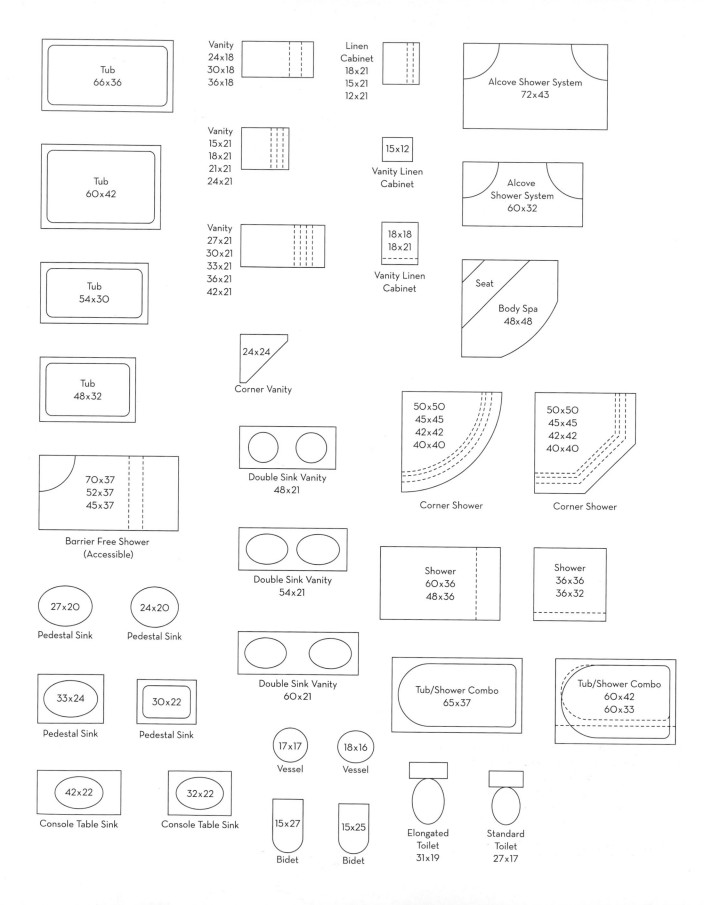

Tub
66x36

Vanity
24x18
30x18
36x18

Linen
Cabinet
18x21
15x21
12x21

Alcove Shower System
72x43

Tub
60x42

Vanity
15x21
18x21
21x21
24x21

15x12

Vanity Linen
Cabinet

Alcove
Shower System
60x32

Tub
54x30

Vanity
27x21
30x21
33x21
36x21
42x21

18x18
18x21

Vanity Linen
Cabinet

Seat

Body Spa
48x48

Tub
48x32

24x24

Corner Vanity

50x50
45x45
42x42
40x40

50x50
45x45
42x42
40x40

Corner Shower

Corner Shower

70x37
52x37
45x37

Barrier Free Shower
(Accessible)

Double Sink Vanity
48x21

Shower
60x36
48x36

Shower
36x36
36x32

27x20

Pedestal Sink

24x20

Pedestal Sink

Double Sink Vanity
54x21

33x24

Pedestal Sink

30x22

Pedestal Sink

Double Sink Vanity
60x21

Tub/Shower Combo
65x37

Tub/Shower Combo
60x42
60x33

42x22

Console Table Sink

32x22

Console Table Sink

17x17

Vessel

18x16

Vessel

15x27

Bidet

15x25

Bidet

Elongated
Toilet
31x19

Standard
Toilet
27x17

Photocopy this grid at its original size or purchase
¼-inch grid paper from an office-supply store.
Then photocopy and cut out the templates on
pages 185–186 to begin laying out your new space.
The grid scale is 1 square = 1 square foot.

INCHES

O   12   24   36   48   60   72   84   96   108

To see more rooms designed by many of the professionals listed below, visit HGTV.com/designers.

PAGES 12–19, SHOWER AMBITIONS

Photographer. Cameron Sadeghpour
Designer/Builder. Haskins Design Group, Residential Designers and Master Builders, P.O. Box 57, 101 Main St., Booneville, IA 50038; 515/987-2277; e-mail: haskinsdesigngroup@mchsi.com.
Resources. *Cabinetmaker:* Medallion Cabinetry; 952/442-5171; website: medallioncabinetry.com. *Sinks:* American Standard; 800/422-1230; website: kitchenaid.com. *Shower system and faucets:* Delta Faucet Co.; 800/345-3358; website: deltafaucet.com. *Countertop:* Midwest Tile, Marble, and Granite, Inc.; 515/334-0139.

PAGES 20–25, FINEST SECOND

Photographer. Cameron Sadeghpour
Designer/Builder. Haskins Design Group, Residential Designers and Master Builders, P.O. Box 57, 101 Main St., Booneville, IA 50038; 515/987-2277; e-mail: haskinsdesigngroup@mchsi.com.
Resources. *Cabinetmaker:* Medallion Cabinetry; 952/442-5171; website: medallioncabinetry.com. *Sink:* American Standard; 800/422-1230; website: kitchenaid.com. *Faucet:* Delta Faucet Co.; 800/345-3358; website: deltafaucet.com. *Countertop:* Midwest Tile, Marble, and Granite, Inc.; 515/334-0139.

PAGES 26–31, CLEAN GETAWAY

Photographer. Cameron Sadeghpour
Architect and Builder. Phillip Vlieger, associate AIA, PineApple Homes, 219½ Fifth St., West Des Moines, IA 50265; 515/271-8175; website: pineapplehomes.net.
Resources. *Accessories:* Abante Furnishings, 515/278-8621; *Cabinetmaker:* Consolidated Kitchens & Fireplaces; 800/888-2667; website: consolidatedkitchens.com. *Countertops:* A.J. Frank Inc.; 515/727-0613. *Flooring:* Phillips Floors; 515/961-7300. *Lighting:* Alpha Sound & Lighting; 800/523-8195; website: alphasoundandlighting.com.

PAGES 32–37, PERSONAL PLAN

Photographer. Andy Lyons
Builder. Kirby Wilmore, Wilmore Custom Homes, 8120 Heatherbow, Johnston, IA 50131; 515/249-3999.
Resources. *Cabinetry layout:* Sunderland Brothers, Urbandale, IA 50322; 800/366-3226; *Cabinetry:* Merillat Industries, LLC.; 800/575-8763; website: merillat.com. *Tile:* Florida Tile; 800/352-8453; website: floridatile.com. *Glass block:* Glass Block Creations; 515/251-6561. *Accessories:* Bed Bath & Beyond; 800/462-3966; website: bedbathandbeyond.com. Pier 1 Imports; 800/245-4595; website: pier1.com.

PAGES 38–45, SAME-SPACE SOLUTIONS

Photographer. Andy Lyons
Designer. Cathy Kramer, Cathy Kramer Designs
Resources. *Window:* Windsor Windows; website: windsorwindows.com. *Window shade:* Hunter Douglas; 800/789-0331; website: hunterdouglas.com. *Unfinished bookcases:* Woodcraft; 800/535-4482; website: woodcraft.com. *Lights:* Kichler Lighting; 800/875-4216; website: kichler.com. *Countertops:* Silestone by Cosentino USA; 800/291-1311; website: silestoneusa.com. *Knobs and Handles:* Liberty Hardware; 800/542-3789; website: libertyhardware.com. *Shower and tub faucet:* Danze; 888/328-2383; website: danze-online.com. *Shower curtain fabric:* Kravet; 800/648-5728; website: kravet.com. *Tile:* Daltile; 800/933-8453; website: daltile.com. *Pullout baskets:* Home Depot USA, Inc.; website: homedepot.com. *Glass block:* Glass Block Creations; 515/251-6561. *Stacking shelf:* Closet Maid; 800/874-0008; website: closetmaid.com. *Other storage organizers:* Container Store; 888/266-8246; website: containerstore.com.

PAGES 46–53, LESS IS MORE

Photographer. Andy Lyons
Architect. Tom Baldwin, Baldwin White Architects, 3939 Grand Ave., Des Moines, IA 50312; 515/255-3939.
Resources. *Field tiles:* Daltile; 800/933-8453; website: daltile.com. *Decorative tiles:* Eurotile through Kate-lo Tile and Stone; 515/270-4920. *Sinks:* Kohler Company; 800/456-4537; website: kohler.com. *Light fixtures:* Artimede through Lamplighter; 515/276-5088. *Toilet:* Toto USA, Inc.; 888/295-8134; website: totousa.com. *Accessories:* Bed Bath & Beyond; 800/462-3966; website: bedbathandbeyond.com. Pier 1 Imports; 800/245-4595; website: pier1.com. Cost Plus World Market; 510/893-7300; website: costplus.com.

PAGES 54–59, BROADER BOUNDARIES

Photographer: Edmund Barr
Designer. Linda Maglia, Studio Maglia; 818/769-7699; fax, 818/769-1271; e-mail: Linda@lindamaglia.com; website: lindamaglia.com.
Resources. *Cabinetmaker:* Vandenberg Cabinetry, 409 E. Gardena Blvd., Suite D, Gardena, CA 90248; 310/324-1175; e-mail: vandenbergcabinetry@earthlink.net. *Tile and marble:* V.M.C. Tile & Marble; 818/363-9776; fax, 818/832-0656. *Bathroom fixtures:* Deco Lav; 561/274-2110; website: decolav.com.

PAGES 60–65, ROYAL TREATMENT

Photographer. Cameron Sadeghpour
Builder. Tyler Homes, P.O. Box 413, Altoona, IA 50009; 515/957-9017; website: tylerhomesiowa.com.
Resources. *Cabinetry:* Mid Continent Cabinetry; 651/234-3300; website: midcontinentcabinetry.com. *Countertops:* Bertini Marble and Tile; 515/222-9600; website: topgranite.com. *Sinks, faucets, shower system, bathtub:* Kohler Company; 800/456-4537; website: kohler.com. *Tile floor:* Flooring Gallery; website: flooring-gallery.com.

PAGES 66–71, BRIGHT FUTURE

Photographer. Cameron Sadeghpour
Designer. Cheri Hausner, Ames Kitchen Design, 2006 E. Lincoln Way, Ames, IA 50006; 515/232-7155.
Resources. *Cabinets:* Crystal Cabinet Works Inc.; 800/347-5045; website: crystalcabinets.com. *Sinks and faucets:* Kohler Co.; 800/456-4537; website: kohler.com. *Accessories:* Bed Bath & Beyond; 800/462-3966; website: bedbathandbeyond.com. Pier 1 Imports; 800/245-4595; website: pier1.com.

PAGES 72–77, ACCESSIBLE BEAUTY

Photographer. Hopkins Associates
Architect. Mark Paul Dinges, AIA, FMR Home Portfolio, 4418 University Ave., Des Moines, IA 50311; 888/937-3939.
Designer. Kelly Dinges, FMR Home Portfolio, 4418 University Ave., Des Moines, IA 50311; 888/937-3939.
Resources. *Whirlpool tub:* Ultra Baths; 800/463-2187; website: ultrabaths.com. *Sink:* Kohler Company; 800/456-4537; website: kohler.com. *Faucets:* Grohe America, Inc.; 800/201-3407; website: groheamerica.com. *Toilet with bidet system:* Toto USA, Inc.; 800/350-8686; website: totousa.com. *Mirror above sink, handrails, shower bench:* HEWI, Inc.; website: hewi.com. *Wall tile:* American Olean Tile; 888/268-8453; website: americanolean.com. *Wall sconces:* Hadco Lighting; 717/359-7131; website: hadcolighting.com. *Glass block:* Pittsburgh Corning Glass Block Products; 800/624-2120; website: pittsburghcorning.com.

PAGES 78–83, RETREAT FOR TWO

Photographer. Stephen Cridland
Bath Designer. Eric Schnell, Alan Mascord Design Associates, Inc., 1305 NW 18th Ave., Portland, OR 97209; 800/411-0231; website: mascord.com.
Interior designer. Tina Barclay, Barclay Interior Design Group, 3 Monroe Pkwy., Suite P-253, Lake Oswego, OR 97035; 503/635-1278.
Builders. Darrel Wallace and Tony Wallace, Wallace Custom Homes, 365 Warner Milne Rd., Suite 200, Oregon City, OR 97045; 503/723-5292; e-mail: wallacehomes@cs.com.
Resources. *Cabinets:* Oregon Custom Cabinets, 503/266-9177. *Stone:* Intrepid Marble and Granite; 503/235-2010. *Cabinet pulls:* Foundry art, available through Ann Sacks; 800/278-8453; website: annsacks.com. *Sinks:* Kohler Co.; 800/456-4537; website:

kohler.com. *Faucets:* Newport Brass, a division of Brasstech; 949/417-5207; website: brasstech.com. *Towel warming drawer:* Dacor; 800/793-0093; website: dacor.com. *Undercounter refrigerator:* U-Line Corp; 414/354-0300; website: u-line.com. *Towels and toiletries:* French Quarter Linens; 503/282-8200; website: frenchquarterlinens.com.

PAGES 86-91, TRADITIONAL POLISH
Photographer. Jenifer Jordan
Architect. William Lipsey, River Studio Architects, 414 N. Mill St., Aspen, CO 81611; 970/925-3734.
Resources. *Cabinets and millwork:* Chasteen Woodworks & Co.; 817/491-4510; website: chaswood.com. *Cabinet hardware:* Baldwin Hardware Corp.; 800/566-1986; website: baldwinhardware.com. *Limestone:* IMC; 800/929-4462. *Tub:* Jacuzzi Whirlpool Bath; 800/288-4002; website: jacuzzi.com. *Brass towel ring:* Jado; 800/227-2734; website: jadousa.com. *Large mirrors above sink:* Inwood Glass and Mirror; 214/351-3553. *Magnifying mirror:* The French Reflection; 310/659-3800; website: frenchreflection.com.

PAGES 92-97, FRESH FACE
Photographer. Andy Lyons
Designer. Cathy Kramer, Cathy Kramer Designs
Resources. *Sink and faucet:* Kohler Co.; 800/456-4537; website: kohler.com. *Hardware:* Amerock; 800/435-6959; website: amerock.com. *Fabric inserts on doors:* Waverly; 800/423-5881; website: waverly.com. *Concrete countertop kit:* Buddy Rhodes Studio; 877/706-5303; website: buddyrhodes.com. *Paint:* Glidden; 800/454-3336; website: gliddenpaint.com. *Window shade:* Duralee; 631/273-8800; website: duralee.com. *Accessories:* Bed Bath & Beyond; 800/462-3966; website: bedbathandbeyond.com. Pier 1 Imports; 800/245-4595; website: pier1.com. Cost Plus World Market; 510/893-7300; website: costplus.com. *Storage organizers:* Closet Maid; 800/874-0008; website: closetmaid.com. *Backsplash tile:* Daltile; 800/933-8453; website: daltile.com.

PAGES 98-103, ZEN TREND
Photographer. John Ellis
Architect. Mark Kirkhart, DesignArc Architects, 1 N. Calle Cesar Chavez, Suite 210, Santa Barbara, CA; 93103; 805/963-4401.

PAGES 104-109, COLOR HAPPY
Photographer. Andy Lyons
Designer. Cathy Kramer, Cathy Kramer Designs
Resources. *Paint:* Glidden; 800/454-3336; website: glidden.com. *Wall sconces:* Kichler Lighting; 800/875-4216; website: kichler.com. *Sink faucet:* Moen; 800/289-6636; website: moen.com. *Tile for shower and floor:* Daltile; 800/933-8453; website: daltile.com.

Fabrics: (floral and green dot) Calico Corners; 800/213-6366; website: calicocorners.com; (stripe) Garnet Hill; 800/870-3513; website: garnethill.com. *Showerhead:* Danze; 877/530-3344; website: danze-online.com. *Towels and rug:* Garnet Hill; 800/870-3513; website: garnethill.com. *Wall sconces:* Hadco Lighting; 717/359-7131; website: hadcolighting.com.

PAGES 110-115, KID FABULOUS
Photographer. Cameron Sadeghpour
Designer. Andrea Lainson, Regency Builders; 515/270-1497.
Builder. Regency Homes; 515/270-1497; website: regencyhomes.com.
Resources. *Cabinetry:* Showplace Kitchens; 515/251-4800; website: showplacekitchens.com. *Countertops:* Centurion Stone of Iowa; 515/727-5998. *Magnetic-back words and images:* Magnetic Poetry, Inc.; 800/370-7697; website: magneticpoetry.com. *Photography display system:* Pottery Barn; 888/779-5176; website: potterybarn.com.

PAGES 116-121, CLASSICAL ELEGANCE
Photographer. Jeff McNamara
Designer. Billy Ceglia, Billy Ceglia Designs.
Resources. *Table, chair, rug, accessories:* antiques. *Chair fabric (towels):* Ralph Lauren Home; 888/475-7674; website: rlhome.polo.com.

PAGES 122-127, SEASIDE SOOTHER
Photographer. Michael Garland
Designers. *Design on a Dime* designer Kristan Cunningham, design coordinator Spencer Anderson, and design coordinator Dave Sheinkopf; Home and Garden Television; website: HGTV.com
Resources. *Bamboo pot and plant:* Bed Bath & Beyond; 800/462-3966; website: bedbathandbeyond.com. *Shadow boxes with sand dollars and starfish:* Michaels; 800/642-4235; michaels.com. *Window treatments:* IKEA North America; 800/434-4532; website: ikea.com. *Chrome soap dispenser and soap dish, white towels:* Home Goods; 661/253-0477. *Black picture frames, chrome doorknobs:* Target; 800/800-8800; website: target.com. *Paint:* Behr; 800/854-0133, ext. 2; website: behr.com. *White floor rug:* Linens 'n Things; 800/568-8765; website: linensnthings.com. *Pendant lights:* Illumination Lighting and Design; 818/986-1383.

PAGES 128-133, SIGNATURE PAINT
Photographer. Andy Lyons
Designer. Cheryl Wasson, Accents & Interiors, 2733 86th Street, Urbandale, IA 50322; 515/334-7415.
Resources. *Large armoire:* Chambers by William Sonoma; 888/922-4108; website: wshome.com. *Side table, mirror, sconces:* Ballard Designs; 800/367-2775; website: ballarddesigns.com. *Tile:* Florida Tile; 800/789-8453; website: floridatile.com. *Faucets, toilet, sink:* Kohler Co.; 800/456-4537; website: kohler.com.

PAGES 134-137, BETTER HALVES
Photographer. William Stites
Designer. Pam Paniello, Elizabeth Saint Marie
Resources. *Sink, toilet, faucet:* Kohler Co.; 800/456-4537; website: kohler.com.

PAGES 138-143, NATURAL OASIS
Photographer. Jay Graham
Designer. Lou Ann Bauer, ASID, Bauer Interior Design, 1286 Sanchez St., San Francisco, CA 94114; 415/864-3886; website: bauerdesign.com.
Resources. *Cabinetmaker:* Andrew Jacobson; 707/765-9885; website: designinwoodinc.com. *Cabinetry pulls:* Bauerware; 415/864-3886; website: bauerware.com. *Solid Surfacing:* DuPont Corian; 800/426-7426; website: corian.com. *Tile floor:* Echeguren Slate, Inc.; 415/206-9343; website: echeguren.com. *Sinks:* American Standard; 800/524-9797, 199; website: americanstandard-us.com. *Faucets:* Dornbracht USA; 800/774-1181; website: dornbracht.com. *Wall sconces attached to mirror:* Peter Mangan Studio; 415/431-7060; website: petermangan.com.

PAGES 144-149, VINTAGE MIX
Photographer. Jamie Hadley
Designer. Gail Pfeifer Karp, Benjamin Imports & Design, Hillsborough, CA.
Architects. Nancy Scheinholtz and Joy Mayerson, Scheinholtz Associates, Burlingame, CA; 650/558-0700.
Residential designer: Claire Beasley, Scheinholtz Associates; Burlingame, CA 650/558-0700.
Resources. *Cabinetry:* Euro-Art Custom Cabinets, Inc.; 415/824-1118. *Cabinetry finish:* Restoration Period; 415/285-0949. *Cabinetry hardware:* Designer's Brass; 650/588-8480. *Sinks, tub, faucet fixtures for sinks and tub, shower fixtures, heated towel rack:* Waterworks; 800/927-2120; website: waterworks.com. *Field tile and molding for floor and walls:* Ann Sacks; 800/278-8453; website: annsacks.com. *Antique chandelier:* Habite Antique Furnishings for Living; 415/543-3515; website: habite.com.

PAGES 150-153, REFRESHINGLY SIMPLE
Photographer. Jay Graham
Designer. David Wilson, Wilson Associates, 755 Folger Ave., Berkeley, CA 94710; 510/883-0868; website: dswdesign.com.
Resources. *Cabinetry:* Richard Klunge, R.K. Designs. *Cabinetry knobs.* Sugutsune America, Inc.; 800/562-5267; website: sugutsune.com. *Tub:* Kohler Co.; 800/456-4537; website: kohler.com. *Faucets and towel ring:* Grohe America, Inc., 800/201-3407; website: groheamerica.com.

to some, inspiration comes naturally.
for the rest of us, may we suggest a good book?

Make that four good books. In all four, including the popular *Before & After Decorating*, *Design on a Dime*, and *Sensible Chic*, you'll find simple and affordable design ideas, not to mention plenty of inspiration from HGTV's expert designers. The newest addition, *Mission: Organization*, is full of tips on clearing the clutter from your home and getting organized.

YOU SHOULD SEE WHAT'S ON !

HGTV.com

HGTV
HOME & GARDEN TELEVISION

HGTV, one of the fastest-growing networks in cable television history, is a one-stop destination for ideas and information for the home—inside and out. Providing hundreds of hours of original programming each year, HGTV offers viewers inspiration and expert advice to transform where they live.

The network—home to such popular decorating and home design programs as *Designers' Challenge*, *Sensible Chic*, and *Design on a Dime*—is distributed to 85 million U.S. households, and HGTV-branded programming is viewed worldwide.

HGTV is an information source across many media, including the Internet on HGTV.com—a premier website for home and garden information, detailed project instructions, episode video clips, and bulletin boards.

HGTV is owned and operated by the E.W. Scripps Company, which also operates the Food Network, DIY-Do It Yourself Network, Fine Living, and Shop At Home.

LOOK FOR THESE OTHER GREAT BOOKS FROM HGTV:

HGTV Before & After Decorating
HGTV Design on a Dime
HGTV Sensible Chic
HGTV Mission: Organization
HGTV The Best of Designers' Challenge
HGTV Kitchens

HGTV Baths:
Your one-stop destination for creating the perfect bath.

Whether you are building a new home or you are remodeling or redecorating an existing space, *HGTV Baths* is your all-in-one resource for expert advice, ideas, and planning strategies. Look inside for these exciting features:

Baths for Every Lifestyle. All baths have similar components—a sink, a tub, a shower—but arranging these elements in various ways allows you to design a bath that serves your particular needs. Featured baths include couples-only retreats, spaces that suit kids or the whole family, and baths that cater to users of all ages and abilities.

Baths Decorated in All Styles. Traditional. Contemporary. Vintage. Asian-inspired. Regardless of the style you love, you'll learn everything you need to know to make your bath reflect your tastes and personality.

Easy Updates. You'll find more than a dozen projects, ranging from simple yet eye-catching updates to hardworking do-it-yourself improvements.

Planning Guide. This information-packed section includes budgeting guidelines, a bath arranging kit, and more.

Ready to create the bath of your dreams? Let *HGTV Baths* show you how to make the most of your time and money—and take the guesswork out of designing a bath that's as efficient as it is beautiful.

ISBN 0696222244-2

9 780696 222443

90000

$19.95
Price Higher in Canada

Visit us at
meredithbooks.com

0 14005 22244 2